How Firm a Foundation

*A handbook on the historical
reliability of the New Testament
and the resurrection*

by

Chad Foster

How Firm a Foundation: A Handbook on the Historic Reliability of the New Testament and the Resurrection
by Chad Foster

Printed in the United States of America

ISBN 1-594676-71-2

www.xulonpress.com

To Wynne and Tricia – the two ladies in my life!

Table of Contents

One of the great difficulties is to keep before the audience's mind the question of Truth. They always think you are recommending Christianity not because it is true but because it is good And in the discussion they will at every moment try to escape from the issue "True – or False" into stuff about a good society, or morals, or the income of Bishops, or the Spanish Inquisition, or France, or Poland – or anything whatever. You have to keep forcing them back, and again back, to the real point. Only thus will you be able to undermine...their belief that a certain amount of "religion" is desirable but one mustn't carry it too far. One must keep on pointing out that Christianity is a statement which, if false, is of no importance, and if true, of infinite importance. The one thing it cannot be is moderately important.

Here is the door, behind which, according to some people, the secret of the universe is waiting for you. Either that's true, or it isn't. And if it isn't, then what the door really conceals is simply the greatest fraud, the most colossal "sell" on record. Isn't it obviously the job of every man (that is a man and not a rabbit) to try to find out which, and then to devote his full energies either to serving this tremendous secret or to exposing and destroying this gigantic humbug?

From God in the Dock by C.S. Lewis

Introduction

In his *Critique of Pure Reason* Immanuel Kant wrote, "I have therefore found it necessary to deny knowledge, in order to make room for faith."[1] Essentially, Kant felt that one must approach religion solely by faith and apart from concrete knowledge. The result of Kant's thinking was a watershed in intellectual history as a gulf was created between the objective and historical facts and the unknowable realm of faith and religion. The Danish philosopher Soren Kierkegaard furthered this notion when he pondered the question, "How can something of an historical nature be decisive for an eternal happiness?"[2] The result of Kant and Kierkegaard is an ideology that downplays the historical basis for religion and Christianity in particular. The ultimate conclusion being that only a "leap of faith can place us beyond the historical and into the spiritual."[3]

While most in our society would not directly trace their own thinking to Kant and Kierkegaard, the consequences of the ideas of these men and other Enlightenment thinkers ooze in modern scholarship, the mainstream media, universities, and therefore in popular thought. That is, the predominant opinion in American culture, media, and universities is that the Christian faith is something purely spiritual and personal and independent to any historical facts and evidence. This has taken the basic shape of the theory that there is a Jesus of history and a Christ of faith and that these two are not the same figure. This is why it is not uncommon to watch a news program that is reporting on Jesus and hear "Well, we must not take the Gospel accounts as history" or "the New Testament was not written to be an actual historical account, it is spiritual book" or while reading an article on Jesus in a magazine we may encounter something like this, "The Bible is not a book of history – it is a testament of faith" or similar comments.

A modern parable that exhibits our culture's blind acceptance of what the popular media presents to it as "scholarship" is the following experience told by German biologist Bruno Muller-Hill:

> When I was a student in a German gymnasium [school] and thirteen years old, I learned a lesson that I have not forgotten...One early morning, our physics teacher placed a telescope in the schoolyard to show us a certain planet and its moons. So we stood in a long line, about forty of us...
>
> The teacher asked the first student whether he could see the planet. No; he had difficulties, because he was nearsighted. The teacher showed him how to adjust the focus, and that student could finally see the planet and the moons. Others had no difficulty; they saw them right away. The students saw, after awhile, what they were supposed to see.
>
> Then the student standing just before me - his name was Harter - announced that he could not see anything. 'You idiot,' shouted the teacher, 'you have to adjust the lenses.' The student did that, and said, after awhile, 'I do not see anything, it is all black.'
>
> The teacher then looked through the telescope himself. After some seconds, he looked up with a strange expression on his face. And then my comrades and I also saw that the telescope was nonfunctioning; it was closed by a cover over the lens. Indeed, no one could see anything through it.[4]

Muller-Hill goes on to tell that one of the docile students who admitted to seeing the non-existent planet later became a professor of philosophy, another a professor of physics, and a third a professor of botany. The honest student Harter "had to leave school and go to work in a factory."

Phillip Johnson used the above story to form "Harter's Precept." According to Johnson, Harter's Precept states that "the way to advance in academic life is to learn to see what you are supposed to see, whether it is there or not."[5] Harter's Precept applies to much of modern scholarship and the media today especially with regards to Christianity. When news-shows such as those on NBC or ABC or when magazines such as *Time* or *U.S. News and World Report* tell us we are supposed to see that the New Testament does not contain an accurate picture of the man Jesus or that Jesus never claimed to be the Son of God or that the Gospels were written well after the life of Jesus by non-eyewitnesses we are supposed to see it and believe it – whether we actually do or not. Thus, when a few of us do speak up we become like the student Harter – sharply criticized and quickly dismissed and labeled as a fundamentalist or something worse.

A classic example of Harter's Precept is the frequent interviewing of a gentleman by the name of John Dominic Crossan by news-shows and magazines.[6] Just a short summary of what Mr. Crossan teaches: (1) Jesus' corpse was thrown into a common graveyard after his crucifixion and the body was probably eaten by dogs.[7] (2) The women's visit to the empty tomb was a fabrication made up by the writer of the Gospel of Mark.[8] (3) The disciples never experienced postmortem appearances of Jesus.[9] (4) The disciples never believed in a literal and bodily resurrection of Jesus.[10] Typically Mr. Crossan's views are portrayed as based on recent scholarship and fact while orthodox historical Christianity is portrayed as based solely on faith. As Dr. William Lane Craig so adequately pointed out in a debate with Mr. Crossan, "precisely the opposite is the case. It is the biblical view that is…supported by scholarship, whereas the theologically liberal picture of Jesus painted by Dr. Crossan is based sheerly on faith."[11]

The mainstream media does not accurately portray the biblical record nor the evidence of the facts. Distinguishing between a Jesus of history and a Christ of faith has consequences for the believer because it tells the Christian that he or she must forsake some of their human reason in order to believe or that desiring an intellectual faith and searching for evidence of one's faith is somehow a betrayal or lack of trust. Even more unfortunate are the consequences to the unbeliever, the skeptic, and the curious. For many feel they must check their brain at the door in order to be a Christian and that Christianity has no intellectual validity or evidence of its truthfulness. Thus, some may never take seriously the claims of the New Testament. The genuine seeker or those considering Christianity need to know the claims of Christianity are authentic and can be fully trusted as reliable – both spiritually and historically. And the truth of the matter is that the Jesus of history *is* the Christ of faith and this can be shown through the principle of *testability*. Using standard methods of literary criticism, historical criteria, and legal reasoning, Christianity can be shown to be reasonable and reliable. The testable nature of Christianity is unique among religions in the world. As trial lawyer, historian, and theologian John Warwick Montgomery notes, "The historic Christian claim differs qualitatively from the claims of all the other world religions at the epistemological point: on the issue of testability."[12] That is to say that only the historic Christian faith stakes its claim of truthfulness on actual historic events open to investigation and on documents open to scholarly inquisition.

Christianity hinges on two main tenets: The historical reliability of the New Testament and the bodily resurrection of Jesus Christ. Since the New Testament is an ancient document one can incorporate the same exact tests used to verify other ancient documents and literature. Upon doing this one will be able to conclude with Dr. Montgomery that, "to express skepticism concerning the resultant text of the New Testament books...is to allow all of classical antiquity to slip into obscurity, for no documents of the ancient period are as well attested bibliographically as is the New Testament."[13] Also, there is much external evidence from other reliable and recognized historical sources and archaeology that corroborate the New Testament record to be viable.

The resurrection event is recounted in these verifiable biblical documents and the content of the resurrection account can also be testable since historical events, geographical locations, and ancient people are mentioned. Further, historical and legal methods can be employed to show that the resurrection of Christ is the best possible explanation for the empty tomb accounts and that the resurrection can be proven beyond a reasonable doubt. All of this means that the fact of the resurrection occurred in actual history, in real time, in a real place, and with real people. Is this not St. Paul's point in 1 Corinthians 15 when he states "If Christ did not rise from the dead your faith is in vain...you are still in your sins...we are of all people the most miserable?" From the beginning the Christian faith has been willing to be tested on the historical accuracy of its message.

The goal of this book is not to create in faith in those who read it. For faith is a gift from God (Ephesians 2:8-9) and faith is given through the working of the Holy Spirit in the Word and Sacraments of Christ and the life of the Church. Establishing the historicity of the New Testament and the resurrection will not prove one into believing. However, this does not mean historicity is not without merit. First, the believer can be strengthened in their faith. For indeed, the believer is called to love God with their whole heart, soul *and mind* (Matthew 22:37). While this book can not do anything about the reader's faith or heart (for that is the Holy Spirit's job), this book can do a lot with regard to the reader's mind. Further, the believer is better equipped to "make a defense to every-one who asks you to give an account for the hope that is in you, yet with gentleness and reverence" (1 Peter 3:15). Another benefit of historicity and the testability of the Christian faith is that the serious and legitimate skeptic can be encouraged and enabled to better understand the viability of the Christian faith and clear up misconceptions and myths about the faith itself. The curious inquirer is enabled to see the clear picture and respond to the very real message of the Christian faith – that God in Christ was reconciling the world to himself.

Finally, establishing the facts and evidence of the New Testament and the resurrection can benefit and challenge the unbeliever. It is too often the case that the rejection of the Christian faith is a matter of the will, or an emotion, or one's ideology and not a matter of the intellect. Too often individuals reject the validity of Christianity because they simply do not want it to be true or because it goes against their already existing worldview and they do not want to have to change their ways. Others simply have an emotive response to Christianity – they hate it and everything it stands for and simply never give the evidence a glance. Overall, many opponents of Christianity have never actually read the entire

Bible (at least seriously and carefully) or they have misconceptions about Christianity's origin and reliability, or they have a personal reason and motive for not wanting Christianity to be historically legitimate. However, if Christianity were an obviously false religion then one must explain the power of its influence, the incredible amount of scholars throughout history who were or are Christian, and finally one must explain away the weight of concrete evidence. Again, regular academic protocol demands that a critic not only provide the criticism and its justifications, but also provide a better solution. The critic does have a burden of proof to bear. The evidence for the two main tenets of the Christian faith (the historic reliability of the New Testament and the resurrection of Jesus) are legitimate and worth investigating, because in the course of doing so one may be pleasantly surprised by joy.

A Bit More About
Historicity and Testability

❧

It is important to emphasize once again that establishing the historical reliability of the New Testament accounts and applying *tests* to the resurrection will not prove Christianity true nor create faith in one's heart. One can not literally prove history nor can a person cause genuine faith in another. Under normal circumstances you can not prove you drove to work this morning – you can only prove beyond reasonable doubt that you drove to work by presenting the evidence and letting others decide the validity and convincing nature of the evidence. We have tools to establish historicity, authenticity, viability, and probability in order to make informed judgments. Each and every day our judicial and legal system decides whether events and accounts of the past were truly historic, reliable, and believable (i.e. "did the suspect commit the crime two weeks ago?" Well, let us hear the evidence and testimony to decide.). Decisions about events in the past are decided as to their truth beyond a reasonable doubt and over and against all other explanations and possibilities. Scholarship provides methods for establishing the reasonability of situations by establishing their truth value. Thus, throughout this book regular methods of evaluating evidence will be employed against the New Testament and the resurrection to see how those items measure up.

Further, this means that a skeptic is no longer able to just dismiss Christianity as something not rooted in thought, scholarship, or fact. Even more so and equally important for the skeptic is that an unbeliever or challenger can not simply refute the methods used in this book or simply state, "I do not believe that," but they must also provide the same methods to their explanations or beliefs and let others decide if their evidence for disbelief holds up under testability as well. So, if one denies the resurrection, he or she can not just say that they do not agree with my methods or refute my scholarship; they must also provide a method that leads to their conclusion. They must also show how their explanation is the most reasonable one. The Christian faith must never let its opponents off from having to bear the burden of their argument as well.

Again, I can not prove the resurrection; however, I can show that the resurrection is the best possible explanation for the empty tomb and the host of other historical evidence that surrounds the resurrection. Therefore, a doubter of the resurrection must show there is a better explanation and why. Similarly, I can not prove the events in the New Testament actually happened, however, one cannot technically "prove" anything in history. For example, there is no scientific proof that George Washington was ever president. We cannot recreate him, bring him back to life, or reproduce his presidency in an experiment. We cannot calculate an equation that tells us that Washington was president. But we can assert with a high degree of probability and beyond reasonable doubt that George Washington was indeed president and was a founding father of the United States. We do this by appealing to historical evidence. Many people saw Washington and some wrote about him. We have some of his own writings and even a painting of him, not to mention his face on our dollar bill. But none of this "proves" scientifically that Washington ever lived or was the president, yet would anyone seriously deny that he was not? Why would no one seriously deny George Washington was ever president? Because the most reasonable explanation to all the evidence we have is that he was. The same is true of the resurrection and the New Testament.

The kind of evidence used in historical research is the same used in a court of law. In a courtroom case certain kinds of evidences are appealed to in order to determine what exactly happened, eyewitnesses are questioned, motives are examined, and the evidence is scrutinized.

By understanding the nature of historicity and testability one can be shown beyond reasonable doubt by using time tested scholarship that the New Testament is a superior, reliable, and trustworthy ancient document. This book will indeed show the New Testament to be such a document and correspondingly what it says of Jesus is also therefore trustworthy. Further, this book will show the true bodily resurrection of Jesus Christ is the best explanation for the empty tomb recounted in those New Testament documents and thus the chief tenets of the Christian faith stand the test of history, scholarship, and evidence.

The
New Testament Documents:
Transmission

ᘒᕮᕭᕲᗒ

C an we trust the New Testament to be historically reliable? This is a crucial question for anyone who is to consider Christianity. How can we know that the New Testament we hold in our hands today is a valid translation of what the original autographs said some 2,000 years ago? These good questions can be answered.

The historic authenticity of the New Testament can be established the same way any document of antiquity is validated. That is, suppose a new document was discovered and it was attributed to Plato or Shakespeare. How would historians and scholars go about validating the historic authenticity and accuracy of the work being legitimately Plato or Shakespeare? The same method used in those cases can be applied to the New Testament (since it is indeed an ancient document). The methodology used in such cases is best laid out in Chauncey Sanders *An Introduction to Research in English Literary History*.[1] Sanders, a military historian, establishes and explains the three-fold test used to establish the historic authenticity of an ancient piece of literature. The ingredients to Sanders methodology are (1) Bibliography or transmission – how did we get the document(s), (2) Internal evidence – what does the document say about itself, and (3) External evidence – do other historical materials confirm or deny the internal components of the document. In his textbook Sanders demonstrates the method on works by Chaucer and other classic antique literature, thus this is the standard method that is applied to any old document whether it is sacred or secular. Let us now apply the tests to the New Testament and see how it measures up.

First, the bibliography test: Quite simply the bibliographical or transmission test refers to the analysis of how a given document has reached us. For the New Testament the question is this: Since we do not have the original manuscripts (called autographs) can we be sure that what we call the New Testament is faithful to the original writings? Or as Dr. John Warwick Montgomery poses the question, "Can we reconstruct them [the New Testament documents] well enough to see what Jesus claimed?"[2] The answer is a "most definite Yes!" In short, the transmission test seeks to evaluate and determine how many valid manuscript copies exist and how far removed they are from the original time of composition. If we can show the handwritten manuscripts that do exist have come to us accurately then we can be sure that we are reconstructing the original and we are well on the way to establishing textual authenticity. *As a side note: not having the autographs is not an issue and certainly no grounds for dismissal. For we have nearly no autographs of any ancient piece of literature. So, if one is going to dismiss the New Testament because of the lack of autographs, then as will be shown in this section, they immediately have to dismiss Plato, Aristotle, and nearly every other piece of classical literature.*

Intervals

Being that the original manuscripts do not exist, the first question in evaluating an ancient piece of literature is "how far apart are the manuscripts that we do have from the original time of composition?" This is an important question. After all, if one has manuscripts within a generation of the original composition and these manuscripts are in agreement, then the likelihood of their validity is greatly increased. The general axiom is the older the manuscript (i.e. the closer it is to the original in date) the more reliable the document. So, what kind of intervals are we dealing with when it comes to the New Testament? Consider the following small sampling of manuscript dates:[3]

THE OXYRHYNCHUS PAPYRI

Beginning in 1898 thousands of papyrus fragments were discovered in the rubbish heaps of Oxyrhynchus, Egypt. The site contained literature, business, and legal documents, as well as over thirty-five New Testament manuscripts. These manuscripts include portions of Matthew, John, and Hebrews. These manuscripts date to early third century (225-250 AD).

THE CHESTER BEATTY PAPYRI

These manuscripts were purchased from a dealer in Egypt in the 1930s by Chester Beatty and the University of Michigan. The three manuscripts contain manuscripts that date from late first century (portions of all four Gospels and Acts) to early second century (all of Paul's epistles and Hebrews. In addition, a third century copy of Revelation 9-17 is part of this collection.

THE BODMER PAPYRI

There are three important papyri in this collection: A circa 175 AD copy of the nearly all of the Gospel of John, a circa 200 AD copy of large portions of Luke 3 – John 15, and a third century copy of 1-2 Peter and Jude.

CODEX SINAITICUS (also designated as "aleph")

This manuscript was discovered by Constantin von Tischendorf in St. Catherine's Monastery near the foot of Mount Sinai. This piece dates around 350 AD and contains the entire New Testament.

CODEX VATICANUS (also designated as "B")

This manuscript has been in the Vatican's library since at least 1481. This codex dates earlier than Sinaiticus and has both the Old Testament and the New Testament in Greek (excluding Hebrews 9:15 through Revelation and the Pastoral Epistles). Scholars have consistently viewed this codex as one of the most reliable to the original New Testament text.

JOHN RYLANDS PAPYRUS (also known as P52)

Since 1935 most of the scholarly world has recognized this

papyrus fragment of the Gospel of John as one of the oldest manuscripts. It has been dated around 100 AD. This is very significant because the Gospel of John was composed circa 75 - 85 AD (thus, this manuscript is within 15 - 25 years of the original).

MAGDALEN PAPYRUS (also known as P64)

This fragment contains Matthew 26:22-23. What is exciting is that recent scholarship done by Dr. Carsten Peter Thiede (a papryologist and director of the Institute for Basic Epistemological Research in Paderborn, Germany) has dated this papyrus to 66 AD. Hence, the Gospel of Matthew was written during the "Eyewitness Period" (the time when eyewitnesses of Jesus and his teachings were still alive).[4]

DEAD SEA SCROLL 7Q5

This is a papyrus scroll fragment of Mark 6:52-53. Thiede has concluded that "it must be dated before AD 68 and could be as early as AD 50."[5] Therefore, the Gospel of Mark was clearly written during the eyewitness period.

DEAD SEA SCROLL 7Q4

This is a papyrus scroll fragment of 1 Timothy 3:16-4:3. Thiede has concluded that, "this papyrus scroll fragment profits from the same archaeological end date as other Qumran [Dead Sea Scrolls] manuscripts: it was deposited in AD 68 at the latest and, by definition, must have been written before that date."[6]

So, what do we make of this evidence? The interval evidence is outstanding and incredibly powerful. Perhaps it would prove beneficial to consider other works of classical literature that are accepted as authentic and look at the intervals of these documents from time of original composition (which again, we have no original autographs for these either) and the actual manuscripts we do have.[7]

Plato: Plato wrote 427-347 BC and the earliest manuscript we have is dated 900 AD. That is a time span of over 1,300 years.

Aristotle: Aristotle wrote 384-322 BC and the earliest manuscript we have is dated 1100 AD. That is a time span of nearly 1,500 years.

Homer (*The Illiad*): Written circa 850 BC and the earliest manuscript we have is 400 BC. That is a time span of 450 years.

Tacitus: Written circa 100 AD and the earliest manuscript we have is 1100 AD. That is a time span of 1000 years. Keep in mind that Tacitus and his *Annals* are the chief historical source for the Roman Empire during the time of Christ. Tacitus is accepted as accurate and reliable and it pails in comparison to the strength of the New Testament evidence!

Another example from secular history to show how impressive the interval evidence is for the New Testament is the Greek historian Arrian. Alexander the Great died in 323 BC and scholars and historians rely on Arrian's treatise *Anabasis* for much of the information about Alexander's campaigns. Arrian put pen to paper hundreds of years after the death of his subject. Yet, no one seriously doubts or questions the accounts of Alexander the Great. Considering that the New Testament was completely written within the time frame of both hostile and friendly eyewitnesses to the events they describe then one quickly realizes how impressive the evidence truly is.

No scholar or anyone who is intellectually honest ever questions whether the books we have by Plato, Aristotle, Homer, and Tacitus are authentic. Now compare the evidence for these other ancient manuscripts to the fact that numerous manuscripts of the New Testament date from 20 – 350 years from the original composition. The New Testament is by far the most superior document in ancient literature with regards to the intervals of time between the original to the existing manuscripts.

Consider how the *Handbook to the Textual Criticism of the New Testament* explains the interval evidence:

In no other case is the interval of time between the composition of the book and the date of the earliest extant manuscripts so short as in that of the New Testament. The books of the New Testament were written in the latter part of the first century; the earliest extant [complete] manuscripts (trifling scraps excepted) are...from 250 to 300 years later. This may sound a considerable interval, but it is nothing to that which parts most of the great classical authors from their earliest manuscripts. We believe that we have in all essentials an accurate text of the seven extant plays of Sophocles; yet the earliest substantial manuscript upon which it is based was written more than 1400 years after the poet's death. Aeschylus, Aristophanes, and Thucydides are in the same state; while with Euripides the interval is increased to 1600 years. For Plato it may be put at 1300 years, for Demosthenes as low as 1200.[8]

Profusion of Manuscripts

The evidence continues to mount as we move on from the interval to the actual number of manuscripts. As has already been mentioned, a large number of New Testament manuscripts exist. Thus, the question is now, "Exactly how many manuscripts of the New Testament do we actually have?" This part of the Transmission Test seeks to establish the accuracy of the New Testament documents. After all, if literally thousands of manuscripts exist and agree, then there is very high reason to conclude they are accurate to the original (especially considering the short span of time from the original to the manuscript).

Again, let us return to our list of four major accepted ancient writers and compare to the New Testament.[9]

Plato: We have seven copies of manuscripts.

Aristotle: We have 49+ manuscripts.

Homer: We have 643 manuscripts.

Tacitus: We have 10 manuscripts.

How does this measure to the New Testament? There are now

more than 5,600 known Greek manuscripts of the New Testament. Add over 10,000 Latin Vulgate, and 9,300 other early versions and there are close to 25,000 copies of New Testament manuscripts. No other document in antiquity even begins to come close to these types of numbers. The second place finisher to the New Testament is Homer's *Iliad* at 643 manuscripts. F.E. Peters concluded that, "on the basis of manuscript tradition alone, the works that made up the Christians' New Testament were the most frequently copied and widely circulated books of antiquity."[10] So, not only does the New Testament have the earliest manuscripts of ancient literature, but it is also the most plentiful and comprehensive document in antiquity. Dr. Norman Geisler based on such New Testament evidence made the following observations: "No other book is even a close second to the Bible on either the number or dating of the copies. The average secular work from antiquity survives on only a handful of manuscripts; the New Testament boasts thousands. The average gap between the original composition and the earliest copy is over 1,000 years for other books. The New Testament, however, has a fragment within a generation from its original composition whole books within about 100 years from the time of the time of the autograph, most of the New Testament within 200 years, and the entire New Testament within 250 years from the date of completion."[11]

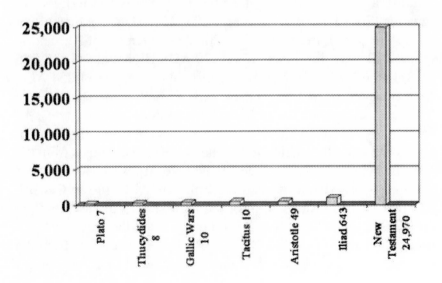

Early Christian Literature

While Christianity may have began as a small movement in Jerusalem, it quickly expanded throughout the Greco-Roman world in just a few centuries. Only two centuries after the book of Revelation was written (a time of Christian persecution) Emperor Constantine essentially made Christianity the official religion of the Roman empire. So, in two centuries Christianity went from being small, underground, and persecuted to being the chief religion of the most powerful empire. During this two century explosion Christian leaders were busy writing letters and books explaining, teaching, and defending the faith.

These early Christian writers (known as the Early Church Fathers) often quoted at length from the New Testament. This is important because it shows the existence and the already established authority of the New Testament within those early Christian communities. These early writings serve as a check on early manuscripts of the New Testament. For instance, if a Christian writer in 125 AD quotes a large portion of the New Testament then we know for certain that not only had that book already been written by 125 AD, but that the book had been around long enough to circulate and achieve authoritative status. Further, we can compare the quote to existing New Testament manuscripts.

Just a brief sampling of some early Christian writers are Ignatius (70 – 110 AD), Polycarp (70 – 156 AD and a disciple of the apostle John), Irenaeus (130 – 200 AD), Clement of Alexandria (150 – 212 AD), Tertullian (166 – 220 AD), Hippolytus (170 – 235 AD), Justin Martyr (133 AD), and Origen (185 – 253 or 254 AD). Now consider the quotations these early Church Fathers made from the New Testament: Justin Martyr made 268 Gospel quotes, 10 from Acts, 43 from the Pauline Epistles, 6 from the General Epistles, 3 from Revelation for a total of 330 direct quotes from the New Testament. Irenaeus made 1,038 quotes from the Gospels, 194 from Acts, 499 from the Pauline Epistles, 23 from the General Epistles, 65 from Revelation for a total of 1, 819 quotes from the New Testament. Clement of Alexandria quoted the Gospels 1,107 times, 44 from Acts, 1,127 from the Pauline Epistles, 207 from the General Epistles, 11 from Revelation for a total of 2, 406 quotes from the New Testament. Origen quoted the Gospels 9,231 times, 349 from Acts, 7,778 from the Pauline Epistles, 399 from the General Epistles, 165 from Revelation for a total of 17,992 quotes from the New Testament. Tertullian quoted from the Gospels 3,822 times, 502 from Acts, 2,609 from the Pauline Epistles, 120 from the General Epistles, 205 from Revelation for a total of 7,258. Hippolytus made 734 Gospel quotations, 42 from Acts, 387 from the Pauline Epistles, 27 from the General Epistles, 188 from Revelation for a total of 1,378. Eusebius made 3,258 Gospel references, 211 from Acts, 1,592 from Paul, 88 from the non-Pauline epistles, 27 from Revelation for a total of 5,176. This boils down to the fact that very early on there were 19,368 Gospel quotations, 1,352 from Acts, 14,035 from Paul, 870 from the General Epistles, 664 from Revelation for a total of **36,289 New Testament direct quotations**. This does not count allusions or paraphrases nor is the total above exhaustive of all the early church fathers.[12]

Writer	Gospels	Acts	Pauline Epistles	General Epistles	Revelation	Totals
Justin Martyr (133 AD)	268	10	43	6	3 (266 allusions)	330
Irenaeus (180 AD)	1038	194	499	23	65	1819
Clement (150-212 AD)	1107	44	1127	207	11	2406
Origen (185-253 AD)	9231	349	7778	399	165	17,992
Tertullian (160-220 AD)	3822	502	2609	120	205	7258
Hippolytus (170-235 AD)	734	42	387	27	188	1378
Eusebius (324 AD)	3258	211	1592	88	27	5176
Grand Total	19,368	1352	14,035	870	664	36,289

J. Harold Greenlee wrote that the early writings of the church are so rich in New Testament quotes and references that, "These quotations are so extensive that the New Testament could virtually be reconstructed from them without the use of New Testament Manuscripts."[13] If there were no New Testament manuscripts nearly 98% of the New Testament would still exist from the early church quotations of the New Testament.

Conclusion on Bibliography or Transmission Test

Even though only one of the three tests has been applied so far to the New Testament it is already showing itself to be an incredible document. The New Testament not only passes the Transmission Test, but it does so better than any document in antiquity. So far what has been shown is that the texts we now possess has a very high probability of accuracy to the original autographs. In fact, Bruce Metzger a Princeton scholar, has shown the degree of accuracy at 99%. In the New Testament there are about 20,000 lines of text. Of these only 40 lines are even questioned (about 400 words). The Illiad possesses about 15,600 lines with 764 in question. This would mean that Homer's text is only 95% pure or accurate when compared to the over 99.5% accuracy for the New Testament manuscript copies.[14] Once again, the New Testament has proven itself to be an exceptional document of the ancient world.

Even more so, the Transmission Test shows statements such as the following one by R. Joseph Hoffman to be naïve and intellectually dishonest or at best incredibly uninformed. Hoffman wrote with regards to the New Testament, "What we possess are copies of copies, so far removed from anything that might be called a 'primary' account that it is useless to speculate about what an original version of the gospel would have included."[15] As has been shown, the New Testament documents are not far removed from the originals and show impressive evidence of being reliably transmitted and copied.

Also, naïve and misleading are reports on news-shows that claim the Gospels are second or third century documents and were written by pious Christians far removed from the time of Jesus and the apostles and that these writers "put words in Jesus' mouth." This is false and completely ideologically based. The facts, the evidence, and the research do not support such a view. The New

Testament was clearly written within the eyewitness period (i.e. every book of the New Testament was written at a time that eyewitnesses to Jesus were still alive and well).

The immediate question is "Why? Why in the face of so much evidence do some portray a picture as quite the opposite?" There are several reasons for such and one of these reasons relates directly back to Harter's Precept (mentioned and discussed in the introduction). If you remember, Harter's Precept is based on the experience of a young student who was honest about not seeing what he was supposed to see. Consequently, he was criticized and ridiculed (even though he was right). Harter's Precept states that the way to advance in academic life or in the media is to see and tell others what you are *supposed* to see whether or not you actually do.

A more current example of Harter's Precept can be seen on news specials about Jesus and the Christian faith done by the major news networks. Much of what one hears on a Peter Jennings' special on ABC or similar programs is based on outdated and discredited scholarship known as the *Tubingen School*. German theologian Ferdinand Christian Baur (1792 – 1860) founded the liberal Tubingen School of New Testament interpretation. Baur applied the philosophy of Hegel to the study of the New Testament. Baur rejected the number of epistles attributed to Paul, argued that Petrine (Peter) Christianity was the early form of Christianity and Paul brought forth a reaction to Peter and a new form of Christianity (in Hegelian terms Peter was the *thesis* and Paul was the *antithesis* and what we have today as Christianity is a *synthesis* of these two).

Another underlying assumption of the Tubingen School was that the Gospels were composed well over a hundred years after the events of Jesus' life and death and were written by Christian editors (redactors) who put words in Jesus' mouth that he had never spoken before. Ultimately the Tubingen School claimed the Gospels were religious myth and legends that had developed over a lengthy time. This thought became quite popular and at the time it originated much of the manuscript evidence and techniques that we have today did not exist. However, evidence and honest scholarship now prove the Tubingen School to be false. We have first century Gospel manuscripts within the time of eyewitnesses and thus there is no justification for claiming the Gospels are legends that developed over a long time in the Christian communities. The Tubingen School assured us of a late second century date for the Gospel of John, but we now have an actual manuscript from the first century. Unfortunately, many books, study Bibles, university professors, and media researchers still make use of the Tubingen School of thought and we as viewers are supposed to see it as fact. The Tubingen School has essentially manifested itself in the 21st Century as a group known as The Jesus Seminar. This group of individuals maintains a naturalistic view of the Bible and the world (i.e. a rejection of things supernatural such as miracles). William Proctor's analysis of the Jesus Seminar's (the neo-Tubingen) view is well stated:

Their hermeneutic (or principle of biblical interpretation) seems to go like this:

Treat the Bible differently from all other works of ancient non-fiction by assuming that it is totally unreliable. So Herodotus, Thucydides, and Caesar's *Gallic Wars* are reasonably good historical sources – but the New Testament is not.

Assume that the supernatural realm doesn't exist – or at least that the New Testament does not picture it accurately.

Assume that most New Testament passages – and especially the resurrection narratives – are fiction.

Rewrite the Bible at will by making up stories to explain away the clear words of Scripture.

Overall, these scholars do have academic credentials. But their interpretations and conclusions appear to be rooted more in personal fabrication and opinion than in hard fact.[16]

This is just not playing fair! It is intellectually dishonest, unprofessional, and academically out of bounds. The Jesus Seminar and the neo-Tubingen school of thought is not rooted in fact, but instead relies on outdated and debunked 19th century scholarship as well as personal ideology. All that the conservative evangelical scholars are asking is to have the New Testament treated like any other ancient historic document.

Often a major problem that arises when dealing with Christianity is that many people and groups simply do not want the evidence to be true! Many want the Gospels to be legends written 200 hundred years after the fact; many want Paul to be a rebel who invented his own religion that stands in contrast and contradiction to Jesus. For if Matthew, Mark, Luke, Acts, and most of the Epistles were written by 60 AD then that would mean the New Testament might just be telling the truth. If the New Testament is proven to be accurate, reliable, and trustworthy then what it says about Jesus, salvation, and sin must also be accurate, reliable, and trustworthy. Here lies a major problem for some – they simply do not want Christianity to be true and so they are willing to ignore viable evidence in order to maintain their own personal ideology. We see this type of behavior all the time in areas other than Christianity. Most people know someone who votes for a particular political party no matter what. Whether the candidate is actually a good candidate, of good moral character, honest, and has the people's best interest at heart is not the issue – the issue is "at any cost, don't let the other political party win." Thus, a person has become blinded by ideology to the point of ignoring evidence.

The next two tests, the Internal and the External, will continue to present more evidence until the only logical and honest conclusion is that the New Testament is an early and accurate first century document about Jesus, his message, his followers, and the first Christians. The evidence will continue to show how schools of thought such as Tubingen and similar ideas are simply not rooted in the facts, but more so in ideology and personal opinion.

The
New Testament Documents:
The Internal Evidence

⌐⌐✧⌐⌐

The second test a historian or literary critic employs when examining a document is the Internal Test. The internal test essentially asks the following questions, "What does the document say about itself? What claims does the document make for itself? What internal evidence is there for the document's reliability?" Here we do well to remember Dr. John Warwick Montgomery's comments on Aristotle's Dictum, "that the benefit of the doubt is to be given to the document itself, not arrogated by the critic to himself. This means that one must listen to the claims of the document under analysis, and not assume fraud or error unless the author disqualifies himself by contradictions or known factual inaccuracies."[1] Another way of putting this is one must first doubt the critic before the document. This actually is only logical. Who is a critic living 2,000 years after the fact to say that the author did not really mean something by a statement? The benefit of the doubt goes to the author and the document and the claims the author makes until good reason tells us to doubt the author or document.

The Gospels clearly claim themselves to be primary source material where the author is either an eyewitness to the events he describes or he is in a position to have these details from a firsthand primary source (i.e. Mark as Peter's scribe; Luke as a companion to Paul). Consider 1 John 1:3 (emphasis mine):

What we have *seen and heard* we proclaim to you also, so that you too may have fellowship with us; and indeed our fellowship is with the Father, and with His Son Jesus Christ.

Or 2 Peter 1:16:

For we did not follow cleverly devised tales when we made known to you the power and coming of our Lord Jesus Christ, but we were *eyewitnesses* of His majesty.

Or Luke 1:1-4:

Inasmuch as many have undertaken to compile an account of the things accomplished *among us*, just as they were handed down to us by those who from the beginning were *eyewitnesses and servants of the word*, it seemed fitting for me as well, having investigated everything carefully from the beginning, to write it out for you in consecutive order, most excellent Theophilus; so that you may know *the exact truth* about the things you have been taught.

Or the numerous occasions in which Paul claims authorship (Romans, 1 and 2 Corinthians, Galatians, Ephesians, Colossians, 1 and 2 Timothy, and Titus).

Again, let us remember Aristotle's Dictum: The original author knows the reason and purpose he wrote something better than a critic who lives 2,000 years later. So, if a document or author repeatedly informs the reader that he wrote about real events and people so future generations might know and believe (John 20:31) then the author and the document are to be given the benefit of the doubt unless evidence tells us otherwise. The New Testament repeatedly claims to be historical and based on eyewitness testimony and therefore the New Testament should be read literally and as history.

It is unfortunate that a literal reading of the Bible has taken a rather negative connotation in recent time, even among Christians. The early Church followed St. Augustine's principle – the meaning of the text is the literal meaning unless context dictates otherwise.

Now days, if someone claims to read the Bible literally they are labeled fundamentalists, 'Bible thumpers,' uneducated, narrow minded, or worse. However, a literal reading of the Bible, especially of the Gospels, need not necessarily mean any of those things or their implications. A literal reading simply means reading the text for what it is and for what it says and the way the immediate context leads you. William Proctor, a Harvard graduate and former *New York Daily News* journalist, states the case well when he writes the following:

> Once the "literalist" label is affixed, the implication is that the individual or group is uneducated, narrow-minded, and reductionistic.

> Yet ironically, a "literal" approach is exactly the approach that the editors and reporters on *The New York Times, The Washington Post,* and other influential urban newspapers want their readers to take. They expect their public to accept every word they publish as gospel – and most of their readers do!

> I cannot count the number of times that I have heard an otherwise well-educated New Yorker make what he or she obviously thought was an argument-ending point: "The *Times* says it's so," or "You really have to read the *Times* today before we can talk about that."

> Also, whenever I would stand in line to vote in a New York City election, it seemed that the majority of people around me were carrying the pages of the *Times* that endorsed different candidates. The clear message was that they planned to vote exactly as the *Times* recommended.

> The point is this: the usual way to read most generally reliable, authoritative types of writing is the *literal* way. This means taking the passages at face value by holding to the primary meaning of the terms and expressions that are used. "Literal" also means not reading something into the text that is foreign to its purpose or literary genre...

So if a section of the Bible like the conflict between King David and his son Absalom is presented as history, it should be read as history – not as a metaphor about family life. To violate this principle would be like saying that a *New York Times* story about African refugees shouldn't be treated as a factual event, but rather, exclusively as a symbol of some more general truth about the human condition.[2]

The New Testament repeatedly refers to itself as written by eyewitnesses and the Gospels in particular claim to be telling the history of the birth, life, death, and resurrection of Jesus of Nazareth. Therefore, the Gospels should be read in that manner. Again from Proctor, "But if we can quote or use *The New York Times* as though it were Scripture, why not give the real Scripture a chance? At the very least, when they read the *Times* every morning, most readers give it the benefit of the doubt [Aristotle's Dictum!]. Perhaps we should give at least the same consideration to the Bible."[3]

A classic example of what the quote from William Proctor refers can be observed in an ABC special by Peter Jennings called *Jesus and Paul*. In the show the theory was offered that Judas was not a real person, but that Judas (the Greek for "Judah") was really a metaphor for the Jewish rejection of Jesus as the Messiah. It is to this type of biblical interpretation that Proctor speaks. There is absolutely no evidence anywhere that suggests Judas was not a real person nor do the writers of the New Testament ever write in a context that would even suggest that Judas was anything other than a real person (so why was this part of a special report on the factual Jesus and New Testament?). To assume that Judas was not a real person is to add to the text and is the equivalent of saying that the African refugee story in the newspaper was a metaphor for the human condition. Honest scholarship allows for the internal claims of a text to be read and understood within their obvious context and literal reading. Further, who would be more likely to know if Judas were a real person – an eyewitness and companion of Judas or a university professor in 2004?

Unless a document shows internal inaccuracies and errors, it should be given the benefit of the doubt. Some have claimed that the New Testament does indeed have internal inaccuracies and errors. One critic was bold enough to suggest thousands of errors within the New Testament manuscripts. Such a claim is a caricature and a gross misrepresentation of the facts. It is true that some manuscripts of the New Testament differ from other manuscripts of the same textual reference, but a look at these differences will eliminate any doubt.

Consider the following:

Manuscript #1: God lvd the world that he gve his one son.

Manuscript #2: God loved the wrld tht he gave his only son.

Manuscript #3: God loved the world that his only son was given.

Could you by comparing these three different manuscripts of the same text ascertain the original meaning? While this illustration may seem very simplistic, this is exactly how the majority of differences in manuscripts are. These are called *errors of the pen* or *errors of the eye* which is what one might expect in a large handwritten book. A vast majority of manuscript differences are matters of spelling, word order, and different tenses. Absolutely no doctrine or central teaching is involved in any manuscript difference. And as was shown earlier in this handbook in the section on bibliography, the New Testament documents have a 99.5% transmission accuracy – the highest of any known ancient text.

Other critics may try to point out what they call contradictions, but in reality they are not contradictions. One example that critics try to point out as a contradiction is the question of how many donkeys were involved in the Palm Sunday entrance into Jerusalem. Matthew 21:2 mentions two animals involved in Christ's entrance into Jerusalem: the mother donkey and her foal. In the parallel accounts in Mark 11:2 and Luke 19:30 only the foal is referenced. While some may try to point to this as a contradiction, it is in fact NO contradiction at all. Keep in mind, the definition of contradiction is "A contradiction is committed whenever propositions that deny one another (contradictory propositions) are both held to be true or both held to be false. E.g., accepting both that "Robins are red" and "Robins are not red" as true is a contradiction." The reason there is no contradiction regarding the donkeys on Palm Sunday is the Mark and Luke accounts do not insist that only one donkey was involved. Mark and Luke simply do not mention the other donkey – they do not deny its existence. The reason Matthew mentions the mother donkey is because he is writing specifically to a Jewish audience and Matthew wants to make sure that his audience understands that Jesus fulfilled the Messianic prophecies of the Old Testament exactly. In this case, Matthew wants to highlight that Jesus fulfilled to the letter Zechariah 9:9. Thus, Matthew, Mark, and Luke all agree that Jesus rode into Jerusalem on a foal. Matthew simply adds more detail due to his audience. Technically speaking there is no contradiction. Gleason L. Archer has written a wonderful book entitled *Encyclopedia of Bible Difficulties* in which he traces every difficult and questioned passage of the Bible and shows how in each case the difficult text or supposed contradiction can be reconciled and that the Bible is dependable and internally consistent.

Hence, the New Testament clearly passes the internal evidence test. The New Testament is a remarkably clear and consistent book.

The
New Testament Documents:
The External Evidence

꧁꧂

The third test of historicity is the External Test. This test establishes or rejects the internal claims of a given document. To state the external test in the form of a question: Are there sources outside the document (in our case the New Testament) that substantiate the claims made within the document? What the external test does is provide and evaluate outside sources to support the accuracy and reliability of the document.

There are many external or outside sources that give credence to the New Testament document. One such source has already been established earlier – the writings of the early church. However, there are many more secular and even anti-Christian sources that validate the New Testament documents. The listing that occurs below is only a sampling and is not exhaustive coverage.

Tacitus

Cornelius Tacitus (55 – 120 AD) was a Roman historian who lived during the reigns of over six Roman emperors. Tacitus is well regarded in the academic and scholarly world as the greatest and most reliable historian of ancient Rome. Tacitus is known primarily for two works: the *Annals* and the *Histories*. In the writings of Tacitus there are two references to Christianity and one to Jesus Christ. The following is from *Annals* 15.44:

Consequently, to get rid of the report, Nero fastened the guilt and inflicted the most exquisite tortures on a class hated for their abominations, called Christians by the populace. Christus, from whom the name had its origin, suffered the extreme penalty during the reign of Tiberius at the hands of one of our procurators, Pontius Pilatus, and a most mischievous superstitions, thus checked for the moment, again broke out not only in Judea, the first source of the evil, but even in Rome, where all things hideous and shameful from every part of the world find their center and become popular. Accordingly, an arrest was first made of all who pleaded guilty; then, not so much of the crime of firing the city, as of hatred against mankind. Mockery of every sort was added to their deaths. Covered with the skins of beasts, they were torn by dogs and perished, or were nailed to crosses, or were doomed to the flames and burnt, to serve as a nightly illumination, when daylight had expired.

Nero offered his gardens for the spectacle, and was exhibiting a show in the circus, while he mingled with the people in the dress of a charioteer or stood aloft on a car. Hence, even fro criminals who deserved extreme and exemplary punishment, there arose a feeling of compassion; for it was not, as it seemed, for the public good, but to the glut of one man's cruelty, that they were being destroyed.[1]

There are several explicit and implicit facts concerning Jesus Christ and Christians who lived in Rome in the 60s AD. First, Christians were named for their founder, Christus (from the Latin). Second, Christus was put to death by the Roman procurator Pontius Pilatus (also Latin). Third, this death under Pontius Pilatus occurred during the reign of Tiberius (who reigned from 14 – 37 AD). Fourth, their teaching had its origin in Judea where it broke out from and spread all the way to Rome. Fifthly, it describes the persecution of the Christians during this time. Finally, Tacitus shows that the earliest of Christians believed in the resurrection (for many scholars who are interviewed in the media today deny the original disciples and followers of Jesus believed in a bodily resurrection). The "most mischievous superstition" is undoubtedly a reference to the Christian belief in the resurrection.[2]

Suetonius

Gaius Suetonius Tranquillas was another Roman historian and as a Roman historian he had access to official imperial records. Writing around 49 AD, Suetonius made the following remark in his work *Claudius*:

> Because the Jews at Rome caused continuous disturbances at the instigation of Chrestus, he expelled them from the city.[3]

The above informs us that Christians had arrived and formed communities in the city of Rome by the year 49, therefore the Christian movement is already several years old by this time (this refutes the notion that Christianity was a later movement that developed outside of the time frame of the original followers of Jesus). And from Suetonius' *Nero*:

> After the Great Fire at Rome...Punishments were also inflicted on the Christians, a sect professing a new and mischievous religious belief.[4]

Rabbi Eliezer

Rabbi Eliezer reflects a bitter attitude towards Christians in his writing believed to be around the 90's.

> Rabbi Eliezer said, Balaam looked forth and saw that there was a man born of a woman, who should rise up and seek to make himself God, and to cause the whole world to go astray. Therefore God gave power to the voice of Balaam that all the peoples of the world might hear, and thus he spake, Give heed that ye go not astray after that man; for it is written, God is not man that he should lie. And if he says that he is God he is a liar, and he will deceive and say that he departeth and cometh again at the end. He saith and he shall not perform.[5]

Rabbi Eliezer is preaching a sermon against Jesus based on Numbers 23:19 in which the prophet Balaam stated, "God is not a man that he should lie." What Balaam foresaw, said Rabbi Eliezer, was "a man...who should...make himself God." God was warning all the peoples of the world through the words of Balaam "that ye go not astray after that man." The claim that the early Christians believed Jesus was God and that he would "departeth and cometh again at the end" is confirmed here in the words of the above sermon excerpt. Rabbi Eliezer stating the movement created by this person has become worldwide confirms the fast spreading nature of early Christianity as well.[6]

Josephus

Flavius Josephus was an aristocratic Pharisee. Josephus was born in 37 AD and died in the year 97. After he survived a battle against the Romans, he served the commander Vespasian in Jerusalem. After the destruction of Jerusalem in 70 AD, Josephus moved to Rome and became the official court historian for emperor Vespasian. Perhaps more than any other source, Josephus provides an immeasurable resource for the people, places, and events recorded in the Old and New Testament. The data shared in this book is only a mere fraction of the wealth of information Josephus provides. Consider the following powerful citation from Josephus' *Antiquities* 18:63:

> At this time there was a wise man called Jesus, and his conduct was good, and he was known to be virtuous. Many people among the Jews and the other nations became his disciples. Pilate condemned him to be crucified and to die. But those who had become his disciples did not abandon his discipleship. They reported that he had appeared to them three days after his crucifixion and that he was alive. Accordingly, he was perhaps the Messiah, concerning whom the prophets have reported wonders. And the tribe of Christians, so named after him, has not disappeared to this day."[7]

Or the following (*Antiquities* 20:200) that gives validity to Jesus having a brother James:

> Having such a character, Ananus thought that with Festus dead
> and Albinus still on the way he would have the proper opportu-
> nity. Convening the judges of the Sanhedrin, he brought them
> the brother of Jesus who was called the Christ, whose name
> was James, and certain others.[8]

Josephus also gives information on Pontius Pilate and John the
Baptist and Herod's execution of "John who was called the Baptist"
(correlates to Matthew 14:1-11).

Pliny

Pliny the Younger was a Roman author and administrator who
served as the governor of Bithynia in Asia Minor. Ten books of
Pliny's correspondences are still in existence today. The tenth book,
which was written around 112 AD, speaks of Christianity and Jesus.

> They (the Christians) were in the habit of meeting on a certain
> fixed day before it was light, when they sang in alternate verses
> of a hymn to Christ, as to a god, and bound themselves by a
> solemn oath, not to any wicked deeds, but never to commit any
> fraud, theft or adultery, never to falsify their word, nor deny a
> trust when they should be called upon to deliver it up; after
> which it was their custom to separate, and then reassemble to
> partake of food – but food of an ordinary and innocent kind.[9]

From Pliny we learn that Jesus Christ was worshiped as a
deity, Christians were people committed to honesty and high
morals, and either a reference to Holy Communion or the early
church practice of the "love feast" or "agape meal." The reason it
is likely a reference to the Lord's Supper is because the early
Christians were suspected of ritual murders or sacrifices and the
drinking of blood and Pliny is informing the reader that it is "ordinary" food and drink.[10]

Thallus

The death of Jesus may have been mentioned in an ancient historical account many years before Tacitus, Suetonius, or Josephus every
wrote. Thallus, circa 52 AD, wrote a history of the Eastern Mediterranean world from the Trojan War to his own time. This document
is no longer extant, but does exist in the citations of others. One such
scholar who knew and spoke of it was Julius Africanus. In speaking
of Jesus' crucifixion and the darkness that covered the land during
this event, Julius Africanus wrote the following:

> On the whole world there passed a most fearful darkness; and
> the rocks were rent by an earthquake, and may places in Judea
> and other districts were thrown down. This darkness Thallus, in
> the third book of his *History*, calls, as appears to me without
> reason, an eclipse of the sun.[11]

From this brief statement by Thallus, we can ascertain that the
Christian gospel (or at the very least the account of the crucifixion)
was known in the Mediterranean region by 50 AD. Secondly, that
there was widespread darkness in the land that took place during
the crucifixion.[12]

The Talmud

The Jews handed down large amounts of oral tradition from one
generation to the next. This oral tradition was organized according
to subject matter by Rabbi Akiba before his death in 135 AD. The
work was revised and completed by 200 AD and this compilation is
known as the Mishnah. Ancient commentary on the Mishnah is
called the Gemaras. The combination of the Mishnah and the
Gemaras form what is known as the Talmud. The Talmud records
the following:

> On the eve of the Passover Yeshu was hanged. For forty days
> before the execution took place, a herald went forth and cried,
> "He is going to be stoned because he has practiced sorcery and
> enticed Israel to apostasy. Any one who can say anything in his
> favour, let him come forward and plead on his behalf." But

since nothing was brought forward in his favour he was hanged on the eve of the Passover.[13]

It should be noted that "hanged" is also used by the New Testament as describing Jesus' death by crucifixion (Galatians 3:13), as well as the two criminals crucified with Jesus were described as "hanged there" (Luke 23:39). "Hanged" is a variant expression for crucifixion.

Gary Habermas points out five key points from this Jewish source: Jesus died by crucifixion, the time of the event is mentioned twice as the eve of the Jewish Passover, for forty days beforehand it was publicly announced that Jesus would be stoned (while not specifically recorded in the New Testament, such is consistent with both Jewish practice and the report that this had also been threatened on at least two other occasions in John 8:58-59; 10:31-33, 39), Jesus was judged by the Jews to be guilty of "sorcery" and spiritual "apostasy," and since no witnesses came forward to defend him, he was killed.[14]

Phlegon

Phlegon, like Thallus, only survives in the writings of other early historians. Origen records the following:

> Now Phlegon, in the thirteenth or fourteenth book, I think, of his *Chronicles*, not only ascribed to Jesus a knowledge of future events (although falling into confusion about some things which refer to Peter; as if they referred to Jesus), but also testified that the result corresponded to his predictions...And with regard to the eclipse in the time of Tiberius Caesar, in whose reign Jesus appears to have been crucified, and the great earthquakes which then took place, Phlegon too, I think, has written in the thirteenth or fourteenth book of his *Chronicles*.[15]

An important fact to note about the above listing of external historical sources that validate portions of the New Testament record is that all the sources are non-Christian and in some cases hostile to Christianity. This fact gives more credence to the truthfulness of the

New Testament because when an enemy or hostile source validates facts (that is, both sides agree) then the probability of the accuracy of the information is greatly increased.

So far, we've seen strong external support for the New Testament from people and books. What about archaeology? Nelson Glueck, a very well known Jewish archaeologist, once wrote the following, "It may be stated categorically that no archaeological discovery has ever controverted a biblical reference...the almost incredibly accurate historical memory of the Bible, and particularly so when it is fortified by archaeological fact."[16] Even more powerful is W.F. Albright's comment as it regards the debunked Tubingen School, "The excessive skepticism shown toward the Bible by important historical schools of the eighteenth and nineteenth centuries, certain phases which still appear periodically, has been progressively discredited. Discovery after discovery has established the accuracy of the innumerable details, and has brought increased recognition to the value of the Bible as a source of history."[17] Below is a brief (certainly far from exhaustive) listing of archeological support of the New Testament's internal claims.

As stated, that which follows is not exhaustive, nor are these archaeological discoveries necessarily significant in terms of the story of the New Testament and the Gospels. However, that is *exactly* why they were chosen and why they provide strong external support. For example, if someone living in the year 2250 read an 'ancient' account of immigrants coming to the United States of America in the year 1950 and the document mentioned landmarks like The Statue of Liberty, Wall Street, and Times Square it would not be that impressive in proving the documents authenticity and trustworthiness because those are very famous landmarks and would probably still be around or at least it would be known where those places once existed. However, if the document were to talk about Spruce Street and a neighborhood that was surrounded by five rolling hills and archaeologists of 2250 in fact uncovered a Spruce Street among five hills then the document would show itself to be more trustworthy. Why? Because the document mentioned seemingly insignificant details that hardly anyone else would notice or consider historic, yet when archaeology proves little details to be accurate it boosts the overall trustworthiness of the author and his ability to describe and record history.

The Pool of Bethseda

There is no other ancient record of The Pool of Bethseda outside of the New Testament. Until the 19th century, there was absolutely no evidence such a place actually existed. Yet, this obscure site with its five porticoes (John 5:1-2) has now been identified. Up until this discovery critics of the New Testament argued that no such evidence of Bethseda was proof that the Gospel of John was written at a much later date by someone without first-hand knowledge of the Jerusalem area and that the pool had a metaphorical or symbolic significance rather than an actual existence.

The Pavement

In John 19:13 the place where Jesus was tried by Pilate (called the Pavement or Gabbatha in the Hebrew) has also been discovered. For centuries this site was a mystery. William F. Albright in *The Archaeology of Palestine*, shows that this court was the court of the Towers of Antonia, the Roman military headquarters in Jerusalem. It was left buried when the city was rebuilt by Hadrian.

Nazareth Decree

In the *Baker Encyclopedia of Christian Apologetics* Dr. Norman Geisler speaks of this archaeological find:

A slab of stone was found in Nazareth in 1878, transcribed with a decree from Emperor Claudius (AD 41-54) that no graves should be disturbed or bodies extracted or moved. This type of decree is not uncommon, but the startling fact is that here "the offender [shall] be sentenced to capital punishment on [the] chard of violation of [a] sepulcher." Other notices warned of a fine, but death for disturbing graves? A likely explanation is that Claudius, having heard of the Christian doctrine of the resurrection and Jesus' empty tomb while investigating the riots of AD 49, decided not to let any such report surface again. This would make sense in light of the Jewish argument that the body had been stolen (Matthew 28:11-15) This is early testimony to the strong and persistent belief that Jesus rose from the dead.[18]

Yohanan Crucifixion Victim

Again from Dr. Geisler:

In 1968, an ancient burial site was uncovered in Jerusalem containing about thirty-five bodies. It was determined that most of these had suffered violent deaths in the Jewish uprising against Rome in AD 70. One of these was a man named Yohanan Ben Ha'galgol. He was about twenty-four to twenty-eight years old, had a cleft palate, and a seven inch nail was driven through both his feet. The feet had been turned outward so that the square nail could be hammered through at the heel, just inside the Achilles tendon. This would have bowed the legs outward as well so that they could not have been used for support on the cross. The nail had gone through a wedge of acacia wood, then through the heels, then into an olive wooden beam. There was also evidence that similar spikes had been put between two bones of each lower arm. These had caused the upper bones to be worn smooth as the victim repeatedly raised and lowered himself to breath (breathing is restricted with the arms raised). Crucifixion victims had to lift themselves to free the chest muscles and, when they grew too weak to do so, died by suffocation.

Yohanan's legs were crushed by a blow, consistent with the common use of the Roman *crucifragium* (John 19:31-32). Each of these details confirms the New Testament description of crucifixion.[19]

Pilate Inscription

In 1961 Antonio Frova, an Italian archeologist, discovered an inscription at Caesarea Maritima on a stone slab which at the time was being used as a section of steps leading into the theater. The inscription in Latin contained four lines. The lines read "Tiberium

Pontius Pilate Prefect of Judea." The inscription clarifies the title of Pontius Pilate as "prefect" at least during a time in his ruleship.

The reader may be surprised to know that critics of the Bible previously argued that the New Testament was not reliable because history showed no record of a Pontius Pilate. Dr. John Warwick Montgomery points out the importance of the Pilate Inscription:

> Modern archaeology – a source of information far less subject to manipulation than literary sources – has confirmed again and again the reliability of the New Testament geography, chronology, and general history...Thus, whereas critics prior to 1961 speculated that Pontius Pilate was a creation of the Gospel writers(!), archaeologists discovered in that year the now famous "Pilate inscription," definitely showing the historical soundness of the New Testament references to him.[20]

Erastus Inscription

On a slab of limestone that was part of the pavement near the theater in Corinth, a Latin inscription was found which reads translated, "Erastus, in return for the aedileship, laid the pavement at his own expense." In Romans 16:23 Paul, who was writing from the city of Corinth, mentioned Erastus and identified him as the city treasurer of Corinth.

Lysanias, Ruler of Abilene

Luke 3:1 dates the start of John the Baptist's ministry to the fifteenth year of the emperor Tiberius (29 AD), while Pilate was governor of Judea, Herod Antipas was ruler over Galilee, Philip was ruler of Iturea and Traconitis, and Lysanias was ruler over Abilene. Abilene was to the north of Galilee and Iturea. For many years the only known Lysanias of ancient history was one who had been executed in 36 BC (some sixty years before the date given by Luke). Skeptical scholars and critics of the Bible at one time used this to assert the inaccuracy of Luke and tried once again to use this as evidence of a late Gospel written far after the time of the eyewitnesses and by people who were not very familiar with first century Palestine.

However, now two Greek inscriptions from modern day Abila have been found which prove there was a "Lysanias the ruler" between the years of 14 and 29 AD. There is an inscription of a temple in Abila that states, "for the salvation of the Lord's imperial, by a freedman of Lysanias the ruler." The "Lord's imperial" was a technical title given jointly to the emperor Tiberius and his mother Livia, widow of Augustus, so this inscription must have been made between 14 (when Tiberius became ruler) and 29 (when Livia died). The archaeological evidence supports the historical accuracy of Luke and shows once again that it is scholarship that must catch up with the New Testament!

Gallio the Governor

Junius Annaeus Gallio was the Roman govern of Achaia. An inscription naming Gallio found at Delphi says that he was a "friend of Caesar" and dates his governorship to 51 or 52 AD. Paul spent 18 months in Corinth, which overlapped with Gallio's governorship. In Acts 18:12-17, Luke writes of how the Jews tried to make a case against Paul in the Roman courts, but Gallio refused to hear it, taking the view that it was an internal Jewish religious dispute. Gallio was executed by the maniac emperor Nero in 65 AD. Why is this important? Because it confirms the historical accuracy of the book of Acts, it fixes a date in Paul's life, and because it shows that the new Christian "movement" was seen as part of Judaism and not something completely new and radical.

Confirmation of the Word "Rulers"

Luke refers to the rulers of the city of Thessalonica as *politarchs* (rulers). Critics formerly cited this as an error stating that leaders were not called by this title. However, recent archaeology has produced seventeen ancient inscriptions from the modern city of Thessaloniki that support Luke's choice of this word (Acts 17:6, 8).

Summary on External Evidence

Dr. Norman Geisler, a Christian philosopher, summarized very well the external evidence test for the New Testament:

The primary sources for the life of Christ are the four Gospels. However there are considerable reports from non-Christian sources that supplement and confirm the Gospel accounts. These come largely from Greek, Roman, Jewish, and Samaritan sources of the first century. In brief they inform us that:

1. Jesus was from Nazareth;
2. he lived a wise and virtuous life;
3. he was crucified in Palestine under Pontius Pilate during the reign of Tiberius Caesar at Passover time, being considered the Jewish King;
4. he was believed by his disciples to have been raised from the dead three days later;
5. his enemies acknowledged that he performed unusual feats they called 'sorcery';
6. his small band of disciples multiplied rapidly, spreading even as far as Rome;
7. his disciples denied polytheism, lived moral lives, and worshiped Christ as Divine.

This picture confirms the view of Christ presented in the New Testament Gospels.[21]

It bears repeating that the brief (not exhaustive) list that Dr. Geisler provides is all information found outside of and independent from the New Testament or any other Christian source! That is, those are facts we would know of Jesus if the New Testament did not exist.

Sir William Ramsay, an archaeologist who was well regarded in his field, expressed how the archaeological evidence changed his view from that of the liberal Tubingen school (such as Acts was a late document written in the second century) to a view of Luke being a "historian of first rank." Keep in mind that Ramsay set out to disprove Luke. After 30 years of in-depth study in archaeology throughout the Asia Minor and Middle East region, Ramsay's conclusions were exactly the opposite of his initial premise and bias. The academic world expected Ramsay to display historical evidence against the New Testament, but instead the world was presented with strong confirmation of the New Testament's accuracy. Ramsay converted to Christianity based upon his research. Ramsay wrote the following:

> I may fairly claim to have entered this investigation without prejudice in favour of the conclusion which I shall now seek to justify to the reader. On the contrary, I began with a mind unfavourable to it, for the ingenuity and apparent completeness of the Tubingen theory had at one time quite convinced me. It did not then lie in my line of life to investigate the subject minutely; but more recently I found myself brought into contact with the Book of Acts as an authority for the topography, antiquities and society of Asia Minor. It was gradually borne upon me that in various details the narrative showed marvelous truth. In fact, beginning with a fixed idea that the work was essentially a second century composition, and never relying on its evidence as trustworthy for first century conditions, I gradually came to find it a useful ally in some obscure and difficult investigations.[22]

To emphasize exactly what a first rate historian Luke was consider that Luke makes specific references in the book of Acts to 32 countries, 44 cities, and 9 islands of the first century and there are no errors. It would do one well to read Sir William Ramsay's book *Bearing on Recent Discoveries in the New Testament*. It contains valuable information and archaeological data that provide support of Luke as a writer and historian and the New Testament as a whole to be a reliable document.

Conclusion on the Tests of Historicity
Without question the New Testament is an ancient document whose transmission is reliable and whose internal and external evidence completely validates the documents to have been written within the eyewitness period. In fact, William F. Albright, the late W.W. Spence Professor of Semitic languages at John Hopkins University wrote the following based on the enormous evidence of

the New Testament:

> In my opinion, every book of the New Testament was written by a baptized Jew between the forties and the eighties of the first century AD (very probably some time between AD 50 and 75).[23]

Louis Gottschalk formulated other tests for historicity, some of which are the following: A document has a high probability of reliability if it is a personal letter, is intended for small audiences, is written in unpolished style, and contains trivia and lists of details. Much of the New Testament, especially the writings of Paul, is made up of letters originally intended for individuals or small groups of people (a congregation). Further, the New Testament is certainly written in an unpolished style (Koine Greek) and there are multiple examples of inconsequential detail (i.e. Mark 14:51-52; John 21:2, 11).[24]

When considering the evidence that results from using standard tests of historicity the most reasonable explanation of the data is that the New Testament is truly a historic book. Consequently, it should be read in such a way and given the same respect and benefit of the doubt that any other established book of antiquity would receive. Indeed, Dr. John W. Montgomery is correct in his assertion that "to be skeptical of the resultant text of the New Testament books is to allow all of classical antiquity to slip into obscurity, for no documents of the ancient period are as well attested bibliographically as the New Testament."[25]

It does bear mentioning that I have not demonstrated that the Bible is infallible or that it is God's inspired word, but that was not the point. Rather, what has been shown is that the Bible's historical accuracy and faithful transmission is impeccable. An individual may still reject the Christian message, but one option that is not available as a basis for rejecting Christianity is the argument that the New Testament is a corrupt document with historically inaccurate information. That is not a sound or intellectual choice – one will have to find another reason.

So, The New Testament Is Historically Reliable. Are They Actually Trustworthy?

I t has been shown that the New Testament is clearly a historically reliable book that was written within the time period in which it describes. However, one can still legitimately ask, "Is the New Testament trustworthy?" For example, one could imagine a document written by a convicted criminal of the first century and in the letter the convicted felon pleads his innocence and describes how he was framed for the crime. Certainly, the letter could be proven to be an authentic first century document, but that does not mean we should necessarily believe that the individual was telling the truth about his innocence. To state the point simply: Just because something is ancient and historical does not mean it is telling the truth – there were liars in the first century too!

There is a way to answer such a question of trustworthiness with reason and logic. When approaching the question "Is the New Testament trustworthy?" it does well to make us of legal reasoning to determine the probability or likelihood that a document (or someone) is telling the truth. We do not know if we will be alive in the next minute or if the next car we get in will start up or if our television set will start when we press the *on* button, but we live our lives as if these things will happen because probability and reason tell us they will. We base most of our decisions and live most of our lives on probability. Legal reasoning is based on getting to the truth and spotting fraudulent efforts of the truth. More specifically legal reasoning is about establishing the probability of truth so as to eliminate *reasonable* doubt. So, let us put the New Testament on trial and see if it shows itself to be trustworthy beyond *reasonable* doubt.

The Simon Greenleaf Test

Simon Greenleaf was born in 1783 in Massachusetts. When the Maine Supreme Court was established in 1820, Simon Greenleaf was appointed the court's reporter. During his twelve year tenure is this capacity he built up his own legal practice and became a large figure in the legal community. At the age of fifty, Greenleaf was offered the Royal Professorship of Law in the Harvard Law School. He held this position for thirteen years. Greenleaf played a major role in establishing the Harvard Law School and it's incredible reputation. Greenleaf personally prepared the original constitution of the African colony of Liberia. Further, he became recognized throughout America as an authority on common law evidence. Greenleaf's text *A Treatise on the Law of Evidence* became a law school standard and citations from it are still found in scholarly legal opinions to this day. Professor Greenleaf took his legal knowledge and applied it to the New Testament and the apostles. In his book *The Testimony of the Evangelists Examined by the Rules of Evidence Administered in Courts of Justice* looks at the trial of Jesus, shows the four Gospels to be in harmony, and that the writers of the Gospels would be believed in a court of law.[1] Greenleaf establishes a legal evidentiary five-fold test to evaluate the Gospel witnesses.

Greenleaf Test #1: Are the witnesses honest?

Can we trust the apostles' eyewitness testimony and the other writers of the New Testament? Are they sincerely reporting what they believe to be absolutely true? There is most certainly every reason to believe the New Testament reporters because they had every reason to tell a different story! Considering the persecution of the apostles and how the early church suffered, the New Testament authors had every reason to review very carefully the grounds for their faith. Further, considering ten of the original twelve apostles died horrible deaths because of their profession of faith, this tends to support their belief in the New Testament accounts. In other words, myths do not make martyrs. Consider the following example: A man walks into a room and puts a loaded gun next to someone's head and says, "In order to live all you have to do is say 'Jesus did not rise from the grave and that Jesus is not God.'" Obviously, we could foresee even believers succumbing to the pressure in order to save their lives. How likely is it that someone who did NOT believe Jesus rose from the grave or that Jesus is God would refuse to make the statement and instead choose death? It seems pretty unlikely that someone would die for something they know to be a lie.

In actuality, the above is not a ridiculous or outrageous example. That was the situation of the apostles, New Testament community, and early church. They could claim allegiance to Caesar and reject their Christian claims of the resurrection and the deity of Jesus and live happy lives or they could remain faithful to what they believed and knew to be true even unto death. A person is not likely to die for something they know to be false, however, people will and do die for what they believe to be true. For the New Testament writers to be promoting something they knew to be a lie would be doing so at the risk of their very lives.

Even more so, the writers of the New Testament were open and honest about their own failures and mistakes and the harshness and difficulty of Jesus' teachings. Therefore, there is every reason to trust that the Gospel writers and the other New Testament authors were convinced about what they were writing and believed them to be true. What they write about and how they write about it are consistent with truth telling and inconsistent with deliberate lying.

Greenleaf Test #2: Have the witnesses the ability?

Did the Gospel and New Testament authors have the opportunity to observe, evaluate, and remember the facts about which they wrote? First, Luke as a physician and Matthew as a tax collector were both in occupations that called for exactness in reports and evaluations, as well as a good education. Consider the following quote from lawyer Walter Chandler, a former New York State

Supreme Court justice:

> [T]he writings themselves indicate extraordinary mental vigour, as well as cultivated intelligence. The Gospels of Luke and John, moreover, reveal that elegance of style and lofty imagery which are the invariable characteristics of intellectual depth and culture. The 'ignorant fisherman' idea is certainly not applicable to the Gospel writers...The fact that the Gospels were written in Greek by Hebrews indicated they were not entirely illiterate.[2]

Chandler's point is well taken. How many intelligent people can you think of that you would trust to remember an important event such as the crucifixion of your master or the healing of a blind man? How many of those people you chose would be able to write a book in an entirely different language very well? The Jewish apostles' wrote Greek incredibly well, thus showing some degree of intellect.

Further, a proper understanding of the Hebrew culture of Jesus' time adds support to the ability of the authors to remember well. Accurately remembering Jesus' words and deeds was not only well within the ability of the apostles and disciples, but it would have been considered incredibly important and part of their Near Eastern culture. As disciples of their Rabbi Jesus, they would have considered it their duty and responsibility to remember and guard the sayings and events of Jesus' life as holy tradition and pass it along faithfully and accurately. While oral tradition is not as prominent in Western culture, it thrived and was part of the existence of a first-century Hebrew.

Finally, one needs only to consult the preceding chapter on the incredible accuracy of Luke in the book of Acts to find that Luke was very capable of carefully observing and recording facts, people, and places.

Greenleaf Test #3: Are there sufficient witnesses and are they consistent?

In other words, is this just one or two people giving inconsistent hearsay, or are there multiple eyewitnesses giving consistent accounts? Consider the following example: Four people are standing near a busy intersection and a horrible car collision takes place. When the police officers arrive on the scene they isolate the four witnesses and interview them as eyewitness testimony. One witness emphasizes how the car coming from the north was traveling at a high rate of speed and the driver was at the same time talking on a cell phone. Another witness emphasizes that the car coming from the south was traveling at a normal rate of speed and that the car from the north seemingly came out of nowhere. A third witness tells the officers that the car coming from the north was going "pretty fast," but then the witness focuses on what happened after the collision. The fourth witness does not mention speeds, but says that one guy was not paying attention and ran into the other.

In the above example, you have four different eyewitness accounts. None of the four are lying, but they each tell a slightly different account based on their perception of the event and what impacted them most. In other words, there are some overlapping facts and some discrepancies (that is, one witness speaks of something that another witness leaves out or does not emphasize as much). This is the case with the Gospels. There are enough discrepancies that support the notion that the evangelists did not sit down and collaborate or make up the stories together. At the same time, there is enough agreement to support the idea that the writers of the Gospels were indeed honestly reporting the same event.

This is exactly what one would expect if multiple honest accounts existed. After all, let us return to our car collision example and when the police arrive all four witnesses tell exactly the same story – word for word. That is suspicious! The only way four independent eye witnesses would have the exact same story and exact same wording and exact same emphasis is if they corroborated their story. On the other hand, if each tells essentially the same story, but with each having different details and nuances then there is a high probability of truthfulness. So the fact that the four Gospels have their own distinctive features and that Mark contains some things that Luke and Matthew do not actually strengthens the case for honest and authentic accounts!

Consider one more example to illustrate the point. Suppose four different people were to write a biography of your life. One is your father, one is your best friend, one is a co-worker, and another is one of your school teachers. Would you expect all four biographies to be identical? Of course not! If they were then these people obviously did not know you that well. What we would expect is that one biography would be from the perspective of a parent, another from the perspective of a close confidant who has shared many private moments with you, another would be from the perspective of you as a student, and the other from the perspective of a working relationship. Obviously there would be points that overlap, but also points unique to each writer would exist. This is what we have with the Gospels. Each writer had a different perspective, background, purpose, point of view, and relationship with Jesus and the other disciples. Differences do not mean contradiction.

Simon Greenleaf summarized it as the following:

> There is enough of a discrepancy to show that there could have been no previous concert among them; and at the same time such substantial agreement as to show that they all were independent narrators of the same great transaction.[3]

Greenleaf Test #4: Does the testimony of the witnesses conform to our experience?

Some might argue that this is the Christian's Achilles' heel. This test is essentially asking, "does what the New Testament describe fit within our normal daily existence?" A critic of Christianity could respond with, "You mean to tell me the resurrection conforms to our normal existence?" In one respect, the answer is "No, it does not. Dead people don't rise to life in our experience." However, what the critic is essentially pointing out is that miracles, things supernatural, or things beyond our current understanding can not happen and are not part of our normal experience. Here it can be pointed out that those things we can not explain happen all the time in our experience. How many times have you heard someone say, "We don't know how he got better. The doctor only gave him a small chance of survival and now he's out playing golf?" Or when a child born pre-mature fitting in the palm of a hand survives and goes on to live a normal life – how often do people say, "It's a miracle!?" How many times has something happened that had no explanation and someone claimed, "We just don't understand it - it's a miracle?" While it may be true that they are not literally claiming divine intervention, they are clearly expressing that something happened that they can not explain. Thus, it is absolutely true that within our experience we hear of things and observe things which we can not fully explain. It is not hard at all to find people who believe they have experienced something supernatural. Thus, when the writers of the New Testament speak of things beyond our understanding it is consistent with normal life.

Greenleaf Test #5: Does the testimony of the witnesses coincide with contemporaneous facts and circumstances?

Legally speaking, this is the chief test applied to the written evidence of a witness who for various reasons cannot be called to the witness stand. Essentially, this test is the "External Evidence Test" discussed in an earlier chapter of this book. This test is asking, "Are there independent outside sources that support the accounts of the writers?" As was shown in the previous chapter on external evidence, the answer is that the testimony of the witnesses absolutely coincides with contemporaneous facts and circumstances (please see the chapter on external evidence for more detail).

The Montgomery, McCloskey, Schoenberg Perjury Tests

Dr. John Warwick Montgomery, lawyer on the bar of the Supreme Court of the United States and barrister in the United Kingdom, in his book *Christians in the Public Square* applies a four-fold test on how to expose a witness for giving known false testimony.[4] Dr. Montgomery's work is based on that of the modern legal scholars Patrick L. McCloskey and Richard L. Schoenberg.[5] The McCloskey and Schoenberg method for exposing false testimony has been labeled as one of the finest works on that subject. The McCloskey and Schoenberg method involves a determination of internal and external defects in both the testimony itself and those giving the testimony. Two of the tests are very similar to the

Greenleaf test already discussed (the two similar tests being the internal consistency of the work itself and the external validity of the testimony itself. This was also dealt with in the opening chapters of this handbook). Since the internal and external evidence for the documents have already been dealt with they need not be repeated here.

The two additional tests are internal defects of the witnesses and external defects of the witnesses themselves. Internal defects in the witnesses refer to any personal characteristics or past history tending to show that the "witness is inherently untrustworthy, unreliable, or undependable." In other words, is there a personality disorder, a criminal record, or some other past history that should cause us to disregard the writers of the New Testament? Were the apostolic witnesses to Jesus persons who may be disbelieved because they were "not the type of persons who can be trusted?" The writers of the New Testament are honest enough to admit their own human frailty, but there is absolutely no evidence to suggest they were pathological liars. Further, if there were reasons to distrust the writers then certainly hostile eyewitnesses and critics of early Christianity would have picked up on them.

But perhaps the apostolic witnesses suffered from external defects, that is, "motives to falsify?" Here the McCloskey and Schoenberg method is asking, "Do the witnesses or writers have any motive to lie and falsify testimony?" McCloskey and Schoenberg put it this way:

> Not all perjurers have committed prior immoral acts or prior crimes. Frequently, law abiding citizens whose pasts are without blemish will commit perjury, not because they are inherently unworthy, but because some specific present reason compels them to do so in the case at bar. Motive, then, becomes the common denominator. There is a motive for every act of perjury. The second major way in which the cross-examiner can seek to expose perjury, therefore, is to isolate the specific motive which causes the witness to commit perjury.[6]

It seems highly unlikely that the apostolic witnesses would have lied about Jesus for monetary gain or as a result of societal pressure.

In fact, quite the contrary is true. The apostles and early disciples lost worldly wealth and social acceptability among their Jewish peers because of their testimony of Jesus. Consider the following quote from United States Supreme Court justice Antonin Scalia:

> The wise did not believe the resurrection of the dead. It is really quite absurd. So everything from the Easter morning to the Ascension had to be made up by the groveling enthusiasts as part of their plan to get themselves martyred.[7]

The disciples had absolutely nothing to gain by their preaching and teaching and everything to lose.

The Givens Bias Test

One should remember how difficult it is to successfully lie. That is, if one wishes to promote a fiction worldwide (such as a resurrected Jesus or the Christian faith) then it would be nearly impossible to keep all one's facts straight in order to keep the story straight. Lawyers and good police officers realize the fact that it is hard to continually be successful in lying. A trial attorney is fully aware of how difficult it is to succeed in effective lying or misrepresentation. Richard A. Givens, a noted legal expert on truth-telling, in his book *Advocacy*, a standard work in legal training from the McGraw-Hill Trial Practice Series, explains ordinary truthful communication and then contrasts it with the tremendous complexities involved in deceitful communication.[8]

Consider the following from Givens:

> The wider the angles of divergence between these various images, the more confusing the problem, and the more "higher mathematics" must be done in order to attempt to avoid direct conflicts between these elements. The greater the angle of deception employed, the greater the complexity and the lower the effectiveness of these internal mental operations. If this is conscious, we attribute this to lying. If it is unconscious we lay it to the "bias" of the witness.

If one is lying or strongly biased, it is not enough to simply dredge up whatever mental trace there may be of the event and attempt to articulate it in answer to a question. Instead, all of the various elements mentioned must be weighed, a decision made as to the best approach, a reply contrived that is expected to be most convincing, and then an effort made to launch this communication into the minds of the audience.

The person with a wide angle of divergence between what is recalled and the impression sought to be given is thus at an almost helpless disadvantage, especially if confronting a cross-examiner who understands the predicament.

If the audience includes both a cross-examiner and a tribunal, the number of elements to be considered becomes even greater. The mental gymnastics required rise in geometric proportion to the number of elements involved.[9]

Dr. John Warwick Montgomery translates the above legal language for the layperson:

Observe that the witness engaged in deception must, as it were, juggle at least three balls simultaneously, while continually estimating his chances of discovery: he must be sure he doesn't say anything that contradicts what his examiner knows (or what he thinks his examiner knows); he must tell a consistent lie ("liars must have good memories"); and he must take care that nothing he says can be checked against contradictory external data. Givens's point is that successful deception is terribly difficult, for the psychological strain and energy expended in attempting it makes the deceiver exceedingly vulnerable.[10]

Thus, the reality is that had the disciples of Jesus tried to engage in lying or misrepresentation on such a large scale (such as writing books, letters, preaching, mission trips, etc.) they never would have gotten away with it! Somewhere along the line someone would have messed up. While it is true that the disciples and writers of the

New Testament never took a witness stand in a court of law, they in effect did take the stand when they began their preaching right in the middle of Jerusalem and concentrated their preaching toward synagogue audiences. Jerusalem was where Jesus was tried and crucified so there were plenty of hostile eyewitnesses in the audience of the disciples who could have easily tripped up the disciples if they had been lying. The fact that Peter and the other apostles were preaching in the midst of a hostile audience who had seen as much as they had adds to the truthfulness and credibility of their message. As Dr. Montgomery made the following commentary:

This put their testimony at the mercy of the hostile Jewish religious leadership who had had intimate contact with Jesus' ministry and had been chiefly instrumental in ending it.

Such an audience eminently satisfies Givens's description of "both a cross-examiner and a tribunal": they had the *means, motive,* and *opportunity* to expose the apostolic witness as inaccurate and deceptive if it had been such. The fact that they did not can only be effectively explained on the ground that they *could not.* It would seem, for example, inconceivable that the Jewish religious leadership, with their intimate knowledge of the Old Testament, would have sat idly by as the Apostles proclaimed that Jesus' life and ministry had fulfilled dozens of highly specific Old Testament prophecies (birth at Bethlehem, virgin birth, flight to Egypt, triumphal entry, sold by a friend for thirty pieces of silver, etc., etc.), had that not been true.[11]

Or as F.F. Bruce comments:

It was not only friendly eyewitnesses that the early preachers had to reckon with; there were others less well disposed who were also conversant with the main facts of the ministry and death of Jesus. The disciples could not afford to risk inaccuracies (not to speak of willful manipulation of the facts), which would at once be exposed by those who would be only too glad to do so. On the contrary, one of the strong points in the original apostolic preaching is the confident appeal to the knowledge of the hearers; they not only said, "We are witnesses of these things," but also, "As you yourselves also know" (Acts 2:22). Had there been any tendency to depart from the facts in any material respect, the possible presence of hostile witnesses in the audience would have served as a further corrective.[12]

On the basis of the Givens Bias test and legal theory: The disciples and writers of the New Testament were telling the truth.

Conclusion

Now that the New Testament has been shown to be both historical and trustworthy, it is safe and allowable to refer to the New Testament as an ancient source. This is the reason that this handbook began by establishing the historicity of the New Testament. Hence, in a discussion on the resurrection the New Testament can be referenced as a legitimate historical resource. This is not the same as using a proof text. I will *not* use proof texts to establish the resurrection because a proof text is useless to a skeptic or non-believer. Instead, the New Testament can be referred to in establishing historic details and facts such as the disciples' reaction and behavior. This is equivalent to a person referring to Tacitus' *Annals* to make a point regarding the Roman Empire or referring to Benjamin Franklin's *Autobiography* when writing a paper on the founding father. In like manner, one is now able to refer to the New Testament to learn of the early church and its beliefs as it has been shown to be an accurate, reliable, and trustworthy ancient resource for such.

The Bodily Resurrection of Jesus

The bodily resurrection of Jesus is not simply a part of Christian doctrine; without the resurrection there is no Christian faith. The resurrection is absolutely central to Christianity. The good news is that this central event is not something one must take on a leap of faith. Far too many individuals, many of them Christians, simply attribute the resurrection as an article of faith and one either believes it or they don't. Quite the contrary, the resurrection of Jesus is rooted in history and the reliability of the resurrection can be defended. Thus, the resurrection of Jesus Christ is an article of faith that can be historically and scholarly reasoned as well. How wonderful, for this is what allows one to love the Lord with all their heart, soul, and *mind*! (Matthew 22:37)

The Importance of 1 Corinthians 15:3-8

For I delivered to you as of first importance what I also received, that Christ died for our sins according to the Scriptures, and that He was buried, and that He was raised on the third day according to the Scriptures, and that He appeared to Cephas, then to the twelve. After that He appeared to more than five hundred brethren at one time, most of whom remain until now, but some have fallen asleep; then He appeared to James, then to all the apostles; and last of all, as to one untimely born, He appeared to me also. (1 Corinthians 15:3-8)

Here Paul records that which he "received" from others. Hans

Conzelmann has summarized why this particular passage has such heavy importance, "Nobody can seriously deny that in 1 Corinthians 15:3-8 we find a formula belonging to the tradition of the primitive church...Paul expressly designates his material as 'tradition.'"[1]

Indeed, since at least the 1960's nearly all New Testament scholars, whether Christian, skeptic, or atheist agree that 1 Corinthians 15:3-8 is actually Paul quoting a creed of the very early church. What now follows is a very brief outline explaining why this passage is believed to be an early creed and the outline is based primarily upon the research of philosopher Gary Habermas.[2]

1. The words "delivered" and "received" (vs. 3) are actually technical rabbinic terms used in the passing of sacred tradition.
2. Paul admitted this statement was not his own creation, but that he received it from others.
3. Nearly all scholars actually agree that some of the words in the creed are non-Pauline terms and clearly Jewish. Such phrases include "for our sin," "according to the Scriptures," "he has been raised," "the third day," "he was seen," and "the twelve."
4. The creed is stylized and in a parallel form indicating it was either an early creed or possibly a hymn, but either way it was written in a form to be easy to remember and recite often.
5. The creed shows evidence of being Semitic (Jewish) in origin, thus predating Paul's translation of it into the Greek. This can be seen in the use of "Cephas" for Peter (Cephas is Aramaic for Peter). And as stated before, the style is reminiscent of Hebrew poetry.

It bears repeating that one would have to search hard to find a *legitimate* argument against verses 3-8 being an early creed. So, the next question is "just how early is this creed?" Again, we shall use dates and facts agreed upon and accepted by scholars, both liberal and conservative, to date the creed.

1 Corinthians was written by 55 AD and Paul had visited Corinth (the time where he "passed on" that which he "received") in 50 AD, thus we have a "stop date" of 50 AD (i.e. the creed had to

precede this date). The accepted date of the creed is three to eight years after Jesus' death. This date fits well with Paul mentioning James and Cephas, who were also mentioned in Galatians 1:18-19. Based upon the Galatians text it seems likely the creed was given to Paul at that time at the meeting with James and Cephas which took place not long after Paul's conversion and within three to four years after the crucifixion. Hence, the creed in 1 Corinthians 15:3-8 is generally accepted as dating around 36 – 38 AD.

The impacts of this early creed are numerous. First, the creed mentions the death and burial of Jesus. Second, it states that Jesus was raised on the third day. Third, it lists several post resurrection appearances and that there were numerous eyewitnesses of the post-resurrection Jesus. But the most important point of the early creed is that it proves the resurrection accounts of the New Testament are not legends or myths created by a later Christian community. Such an early creed confessing these facts makes it impossible for the resurrection of Jesus to be dismissed as a legend or myth. It would take at least two generations (if not more) for a legend to begin to develop and then replace and erase historical facts. There is no way for a legend to have already taken root within three to eight years after the event in question because the presence of living hostile witnesses would not have allowed it. The early creed shows that the death, burial, and bodily resurrection of Jesus were part of the apostles and the early church's first confession.

The Evidence and the Case for the Resurrection

As has been discussed and alluded to earlier and throughout the book, there are certain historic facts agreed upon by virtually all historians and New Testament scholars (and this is wonderful because it eliminates the debate over some issues and allows for a common ground or starting point). Making use of just four of these *facts of consensus* the resurrection of Jesus proves to be the most reasonable explanation to the known and accepted facts. Further, all explanations against a bodily resurrection of Jesus either contradict these known and accepted historical facts or they refuse to deal with them. Any explanation or proof of the resurrection (or disproof) must be consistent with and fit within the framework of the following four historical accepted facts.

Fact #1: Jesus was crucified, died, and was then buried in the tomb of Joseph of Arimethea.

The fact that Jesus was crucified is almost universally accepted. This is because not only does the New Testament, a historically reliable document, record and describe the event, but numerous other historically reliable sources speak of Jesus of Nazareth as being crucified. Some of these extra-biblical, secular sources include Tacitus, Pliny the Younger, Suetonius, Thallus, Phlegon, Lucian of Samosata, the Jewish Talmud, and Josephus. These sources are from Roman and Jewish sources – all hostile toward Christianity (or at the very least not Christian nor sympathetic to the Christian cause).

It would almost seem to be a moot point to say that Jesus died if we know that he was crucified. However, some have tried to argue that Jesus did not really die on the cross and that is how he was able to fake a resurrection. Jesus surviving is highly unlikely. A university professor once quibbled that if you believe that Jesus survived the crucifixion then you really should have no problem believing in anything the Bible says because it takes more faith to believe Jesus survived the cross! In the March 21, 1986 edition of the *Journal of the American Medical Association* a physician by the name of William D. Edwards studied the crucifixion from a medical standpoint. Dr. Edwards made use of the available descriptions of Jesus' crucifixion as well as all historical and archeological information about Roman crucifixions at the time of Jesus. The article goes into incredible depth and reaches the following conclusion:

> Clearly the weight of historical and medical evidence indicates that Jesus was dead before the wound to his side was inflicted and supports the traditional view that the spear, thrust between his right ribs, probably perforated not only the right lung, but also the pericardium and heart and thereby ensured his death. Accordingly, interpretations based on the assumption that Jesus did not die on the cross appear to be at odds with modern medical knowledge.[3]

Further, keep in mind that the Romans were not new to crucifixions. It was not as if Jesus were one of the first few cases of crucifixion. The Romans had professional executors who were trained and had been crucifying the convicted for quite a period of time, thus they knew exactly what they were doing and how to do it well.

Jesus was crucified, he died, and now it will be established that he was buried in a known location in the tomb of Joseph of Arimathea. There are at least six main points that support the burial of Jesus in a known tomb by Joseph of Arimathea. First, the pre-Pauline creed of 1 Corinthians 15:3 – 8 mentions the burial. As established earlier, it is virtually universally acknowledged that Paul is citing a primitive creed in 1 Corinthians 15 dating around 33 – 38 AD. Further, the tradition which Paul cites in 1 Corinthians focused mostly on Jerusalem-based disciples (Cephas [Peter], James, and the Twelve), and in this situation, it becomes difficult to imagine that Paul did not discuss the account of the Passion of Jesus which would have certainly included the death, the burial, and the resurrection in some depth. Indeed, C.H. Dodd had it right when he humorously wrote, "We may presume they did not spend all their time talking about the weather."[4]

Second, Mark's account of the burial is simple in its basic elements and is not heavily imbued with theology. Joseph of Arimathea asks for the body of Jesus, it is granted to him, Joseph has it wrapped, and lays it in a tomb. Even the liberal theologian Rudolph Bultmann (who argued that most of the New Testament was myth) agreed to this point.

Third, Joseph of Arimathea is described as a member of the Sanhedrin which, according to Mark, unanimously voted to condemn Jesus to death (Mark 14:55, 64; 15:1 and remember the New Testament is a historical accurate book). Thus, Joseph of Arimathea is highly unlikely to be a Christian invention. Mark describes Joseph of Arimathea as a *prominent* member of the Sanhedrin. Being that Joseph is a prominent member, then he would be well known. Thus, if Joseph were an invention then surely someone with ties to the Sanhedrin would have exploited this. That is, someone close to the Sanhedrin could have said something similar to the following, "My uncle was on the Sanhedrin, and he doesn't remember any prominent member named Joseph."

Fourth, the Jews always buried their dead - even the most despicable and criminal among them and also the dead of their enemies. See Tobit 1:17-19; 2:3-7; 12:12-13; Sirach 7:33; 38:16, Joshua 8:29; 10:27, and most importantly Deuteronomy 21:22-23 for references to the fact that the Jews took seriously the burial of the dead. The Deuteronomy passage speaks of not letting one who has "hung on a tree" remain dead on the tree overnight. "Hung on a tree" is a biblical metaphor for crucifixion. Further, in regards to crucifixion, the Temple Scroll (IIQ Temple) records a command to bury the body of one who has been crucified on the same day. Lastly, Josephus the Jewish historian mentions the command to bury on the same day one who has been hung on a tree after being stoned to death in a first-century context and Josephus mentions the Deuteronomy 21:22-33 passage within this account (*Antiquities* 4. 202 and *Jewish War* 4. 317). From Josephus:

> The Jews are so careful about funeral rites that even malefactors who have been sentenced to crucifixion are taken down and buried before sunset.[5]

All of this naturally fits with the New Testament Gospel descriptions. For instance in Matthew 27:57ff it describes Joseph of Arimathea going to Pilate at evening to get the body down from the cross and John 19:31ff where it describes the Jews asking Pilate to take the bodies off of the crosses. Quite simply, first century Jewish attitudes toward burial give every reason to believe Jesus was also buried. Also, consider that it is Passover week in Jerusalem and tension is at an all time high. Pilate certainly did not want a riot on his hands and desecrating a dead Jewish body (even one of a criminal) would have sent the Jews into upheaval. Anyone denying the burial of Jesus by Joseph of Arimathea holds the burden of proof. They are going to have to have some very serious concrete evidence on why Jesus was an exception to centuries of Jewish custom and so far no such evidence has been presented.

Fifth, the women's witnessing the burial is a believable account from the Gospels. Women were not allowed to give legal testimony and their social status in first century Judaism was very low to say the least. Women being used as witnesses in spite of their counter-productive status give credence to the account.

Sixth, no other burial tradition exists. If the Gospel writers invented the tomb burial by Joseph of Arimathea, one should expect competition to this tradition by the true sequence of events, a competitive group, those seeking fame and fortune, or Jewish polemic. But as Matthew's account of the guarding of the tomb tells us, the Jewish polemic presupposed that Jesus' body was buried in a tomb at a location of which was known and no other traditions have ever been discovered.

It is for these reasons that scholars such as William Lane Craig and A.T. Roberts of Cambridge University have concluded that "the burial of Jesus is one of the most certain facts about the historical Jesus...[Jesus burial] is one of the earliest and best-attested facts about Jesus."[6]

Fact #2: The tomb of Jesus was found empty on the Sunday after the crucifixion.

Remember, we are building a case here. First, we have just established that Jesus was crucified, died, and then he was buried in a known location. Now, it is necessary to establish that the known tomb was found empty on the Sunday after the crucifixion. In so doing anyone looking at the evidence will then be forced to ask the question, "If we know he died and we know he was buried and we know the tomb was found empty three days later, then what happened to the body?"

The obvious point about the empty tomb: The Jewish leaders who were part of the plan to crucify Jesus and who saw him cruci-fied would have loved to been able to say, "Look, this is the tomb, we all know this is where Joseph of Arimethea put Jesus, and here is the body – still as dead as ever!" Had they been able to do so, Christianity would never have been born. Yet, no such record exists.

Second, since we have established the New Testament as a reli-able and trustworthy historical source then consider what it states about the tomb on the Sunday after Good Friday. The New Testament states that there were many eyewitnesses of a living

Jesus after that first Easter Sunday – literally hundreds of them over a span of forty days. 1 Corinthians 15:6 states"... He was seen by over five hundred brethren at once ...". John 20:10-31 also recounts the fact that many individuals saw Jesus after His death on the cross. Not only that, but His followers were so committed to this truth that they preached the empty tomb at every possible opportunity even risking their own lives to do so. The New Testament explicitly states that Jesus' gravestone had been moved and that Jesus' body was missing (Matthew 28).

Third, consider the fact that the resurrection was almost immediately preached in the city of Jerusalem. Why is this such an important fact? Jesus' disciples did not go to some obscure place where no one had heard of Jesus to begin preaching about the resurrection, rather they began preaching in Jerusalem, the very city where Jesus had died and been buried. The disciples could not have done this unless it was a common fact that the tomb was found empty or else all those hostile witnesses in Jerusalem who saw the events of Passion Week and who knew where the tomb was could have easily squashed such preaching. Paul Althaus correctly and logically observes that the resurrection proclamation "could not have been maintained in Jerusalem for a single day, for a single hour, if the emptiness of the tomb had not been established as a fact for all concerned."[7] Similarly, William Lane Craig has written the following:

> When therefore the disciples began to preach the resurrection in Jerusalem and people responded, and when the religious authorities stood helplessly by, the tomb must have been empty. The simple fact that the Christian fellowship, founded on belief in Jesus' resurrection, came into existence and flourished in the very city where he was executed and buried is powerful evidence for the historicity of the empty tomb.[8]

Fourth, the earliest Jewish arguments against Christianity admit the empty tomb. When the most hostile of witnesses concurs then one can feel most certain that the issue at hand is true. Dr. Paul Maier refers to this as "positive evidence from a hostile source. In essence, if a source admits a fact that is decidedly not in its favor, the fact is genuine."[9] In Matthew 28:11-15, there is a reference made to the Jew's attempt to refute Christianity by saying that the disciples stole the body. Again this shows that the Jews did not deny the empty tomb. Instead, their "stolen body" theory admitted the significant truth that the tomb was in fact found empty. The *Toledoth Jesu*, a compilation of early Jewish writings, is another source acknowledging the empty tomb with an explanation for it.

Fifth, as the empty tomb and resurrection were an immediate part of the Christian faith and creed as was shown at the beginning of this chapter regarding 1 Corinthians 15:3 – 8, thus there was not enough time for a legend or myth to develop and spread. Further, the Gospels' accounts of the empty tomb are simple and show no signs of legendary development. This is obvious when one compares the Gospels of the New Testament with the Gospel of Peter, a forgery from about 125 AD. The Gospel of Peter has all of the Jewish leaders, Roman guards, and many people from the countryside gathered to watch the resurrection. Then three men come out of the tomb, with their heads reaching up to the clouds. Then a talking cross comes out of the tomb. This is what legend looks like and such embellishments are not found in the New Testament.

Sixth, Jesus' tomb was never venerated as a shrine. This is striking because it was a custom of first century Judaism to set up a shrine at the site of a holy man's bones. There were at least 50 such sites in Jesus' day. Since there was no such shrine for Jesus, it suggests that his disciples and those who would have considered him holy knew that his bones were not there.

Consider the following quotes from reliable and noteworthy theologians:

Paul Maier: "[I]f all the evidence is weighed carefully and fairly, it is indeed justifiable, according to the canons of historical research, to conclude that the sepulcher of Joseph of Arimathea, in which Jesus was buried, was actually empty on the morning of the first Easter. And no shred of evidence has yet been discovered in literary sources, epigraphy, or archaeology that would disprove this statement."[10]

D.H. Van Daalen: "It is extremely difficult to object to the empty tomb on historical grounds; those who deny it do so on the basis of theological or philosophical assumptions."[11]

Jacob Kremer, who has specialized in the study of the resurrection and is a New Testament critic wrote "By far most exegetes hold firmly to the reliability of the biblical statements about the empty tomb."[12] Kremer then goes on to list twenty-eight scholars to back up his statement.

Fact #3: On independent multiple occasions and to multiple eyewitnesses, disciples of Jesus saw what they firmly believed to be genuine appearances of Jesus alive from the dead.

Keeping in mind the theme of building a case: It has been established by the evidence that Jesus was crucified, that he died, that he was buried, and that the known tomb was found empty three days later. What happened to the body? Well, there is evidence that Jesus' disciples had real experiences with one whom they believed was the risen Christ. The previous statement is actually not disputed as much as one might suspect. The main reason is because of the wording, in particular "with one whom they believed was the risen Christ." Again, one can look not only to the Gospels for this, but also that 1 Corinthians 15:3 – 8 passage quoting the earliest known creed of the Church (within a few years of Jesus' death itself).

> For I delivered to you as of first importance what I also received, that Christ died for our sins according to the Scriptures, and that He was buried, and that He was raised on the third day according to the Scriptures, and that He appeared to Cephas, then to the twelve. After that He appeared to more than five hundred brethren at one time.

Now, in all fairness it must be acknowledged that just because the disciples believed that they saw Jesus does not mean that they really did. However, there are only three possibilities:

1. The disciple were lying

2. The disciples had hallucinations of Jesus
3. The disciples really saw the risen Christ

The task now is to decide which of the three options is the most likely and the most supported by the known facts and history. First, were the disciples lying? If the disciples were lying then they knew full well that Jesus had not really risen, but they made up the story of the resurrection. While at first one may be attracted to this explanation or find it possible, a full understanding of the implications and psychology of the disciples ultimately rules out this possibility. Quite simply, myths do not make martyrs. People do not die for something they know to be a lie. A person may die for a lie, but they die believing the lie to be truth. It is really unlikely to view the disciples as choosing horrible deaths and persecution to promote something they know is an absolute lie. Would you or anyone you know die to promote something you know is absolutely false? It is for this reason that hardly anyone accepts the notion that the disciples were outright lying about the resurrection and making up the whole thing. Thus, skeptics concede that the disciples "believed they had real experiences with the risen Jesus."

Were the disciples hallucinating or having fantastic visions brought about by deep religious conviction or psychologically induced fantasies? The hallucination theory is also not a viable option because it cannot explain away the physical nature of the appearances. The New Testament (a historically reliable document) records eating and drinking with Jesus, as well as touching him. Dead men do not eat fish. John emphasized "touch" in his epistles. This cannot be done with hallucinations. Second, it is highly unlikely that all the disciples would have had the exact same hallucination. Hallucinations, visions, and psychologically induced fantasies are highly individual and not group projections. The hallucination theory would basically be the same as saying, "wasn't that a great dream I had last night?" Chances are you have never had the same dream as someone else. Even more so, the so called hallucinations would have had to occur to over 500 different people at different places over a period of forty days. Obviously this is not very likely or possible. Further, the hallucination theory cannot explain the conversion of Paul three years later (which is another accepted fact – Saul of Tarsus converted). How could or why would Paul, the persecutor of Christians, so desire to see the resurrected Jesus whom he did not believe in that his mind invented an appearance as well? Finally, the evidence must also be consistent with prior established facts. Thus, how can the hallucination theory deal with the very real evidence for the empty tomb? Hallucination is ruled out as a possibility.

Since the apostles and other disciples were not lying nor were they hallucinating, then the only possible explanation left for the reason that the disciples *believed* that they had seen the risen Jesus is because they really had seen and encountered the risen Jesus.

Fact #4: The incredible transformation of the disciples.

There was something that made the disciples of Jesus change from being cowards hiding in an upper room afraid for their lives to being bold enough to stand up in front of thousands of people and proclaim that Jesus was alive. Simply compare the apostles, Peter in particular, as described in the Gospels to the difference in their behavior and actions after the resurrection in the book of Acts. The only reasonable explanation for such a transformation was the deep conviction that Jesus had risen from the grave. In addition, this transformation was not short lived, but continued to thrive in the face of persecution and death and still survives today. The apostles and disciples were willing to be punished, imprisoned, beaten, rejected, and even killed for their confession of faith that Jesus had risen from the dead (see Acts 16:22; 2 Corinthians 11:23 - 27).

In the religion section of *Time Magazine,* May 7, 1979, it was reported that an Orthodox Jewish rabbi had written a book claiming that the bodily resurrection of Jesus was a true historical event. The rabbi's name was Pinchas Lapide. What is even more shocking is that the rabbi did not become a Christian, however, he was at least being honest with the facts in admitting that the evidence for the resurrection was overwhelming and simply could not be denied. Ultimately, the rabbi concluded that God raised Jesus from the dead, not because Jesus was the Messiah, but out of mercy. Rabbi Lapide wrote a book called *The Resurrection of Jesus: A Jewish*

Perspective. If only all non-Christians could be as honest with the evidence for the resurrection as Rabbi Lapide. In his book the rabbi wrote the following:

> When this scared, frightened band of apostles which was just about to throw away everything in order to flee in despair to Galilee; when these peasants, shepherds, and fishermen, who betrayed and denied their master and failed him so miserably, suddenly could be changed overnight into a confident mission society, convinced of salvation and able to work with much more success after Easter than before, then no vision or hallucination is sufficient to explain such a revolutionary transformation.[13]

John Stott wrote the following:

> Perhaps the transformation of the disciples of Jesus is the greatest evidence for the resurrection. It was the resurrection which transformed Peter's fear into courage, and James' doubt into faith. It was the resurrection which changed the Sabbath into Sunday and the Jewish remnant into the Christian Church. It was the resurrection which changed Saul the Pharisee into Paul the Apostle and turned his persecuting into preaching.[14]

The disciples' transformation could not have arisen without an objective event or reality as a catalyst and that reality was the resurrected Jesus.

Other facts:

The four facts described above are the most compelling, however, other accepted facts do exist (for example, Gary Habermas has a list of twelve facts that both he and the skeptics of the resurrection that he debates agree upon as historic facts). Another fact that deserves consideration is the emergence of the Christian church. Lee Strobel wrote that, "When a major cultural shift takes place, historians always look for events that can explain it. There's no question that these culture shifts began shortly after the death of Jesus and spread so rapidly that within a period of maybe twenty years it had even reached Caesar's palace in Rome."[15] Dr. James McCullen put it this way, "If you were a Martian looking down on the first century, would you think Christianity or the Roman Empire would survive? You probably wouldn't put money on a ragtag group of people whose primary message was that a crucified carpenter from an obscure village had triumphed over the grave. Yet it was so successful that today we name our children Peter and Paul and our dogs Caesar and Nero!"[16] The emergence of the Church, its prospering success in spite of seeming odds against it, and continued existence today can only find a satisfactory explanation in the life, death, and resurrection of Jesus as described in the New Testament. The Church is a concrete fact of history and the explanation for its existence and persistence is the resurrection of Jesus of Nazareth.

One more fact to consider is the emergence of Sunday as becoming the day of worship. The apostles and most of the earliest Church were Jews. In the book of Genesis the Sabbath was the celebration of God's work in the creation process (see Genesis 2:2-3; Exodus 20:11). After the Exodus the Sabbath was expanded to include a celebration and remembrance of God's deliverance and redemption (see Deuteronomy 5:15). Observance of the Sabbath was high on the religious priority and obligation list for first century Jews. In other words, it would have taken something almost beyond imagination for a first century Jew to consider adding, changing, or tampering with the Sabbath in any way, shape, or form. However, that is exactly what many first century Jews did. The Jewish Christians succeeded in moving to Sunday the theologically packed day of rest and worship. What could have possibly motivated Jews to do this, Jews who understood the implications of the Sabbath? The resurrection. Along these lines, the sacrificial system and circumcision which were also a key part of first century Judaism were quickly ended and replaced by the sacraments of the Church – The Lord's Supper and Holy Baptism. Sacrifices were no longer necessary for the Jewish Christians and Passover, ceremonial washing, and the covenant of circumcision were replaced with Communion and Baptism into the name of the Father, Son, and Holy Spirit. Only an event that would have previously been beyond words could have motivated sincere first century Jews to cease temple sacrifices and circumcision and to replace it with something they believed to the be the better fulfillment of such acts. That event was the resurrection of Jesus.

Competing Theories:[17]

As has already been shown, the hallucination theory is not possible nor is the theory that Jesus did not actually die on the cross (the Swoon theory) nor is the theory that the resurrection was a later legend that developed. However, there are a few more possibilities to consider and logically rule out. One such theory against the resurrection is that the disciples went to the wrong tomb. Perhaps due to their emotional condition and the darkness, the women visited the wrong tomb. Overjoyed to see that it was empty, they rushed back to tell the disciples Jesus had risen and then the disciples in turn ran into Jerusalem to proclaim the Resurrection. There are several major flaws with this explanation. First, it is extremely doubtful that the Apostles would not have corrected the women's error. The Gospel of John gives a very detailed account of them doing just that. Second, as was shown earlier the tomb site was known not only by the followers of Christ but also by their opponents. The Gospels make it clear the body was buried in the tomb of Joseph of Arimathea, a prominent member of the Jewish council. If the body still remained in the tomb while the Apostles began preaching, the authorities simply would have gone to the right tomb, produced the body, and marched it down the streets. This would have ended the Christian faith once and for all. Remember, the preaching of the Resurrection began in Jerusalem, fifteen minutes away from the crucifixion site and the tomb. These factors make this theory extremely weak.

Another theory is the stolen body theory. This theory suggests that either Jewish and/or Roman authorities stole the body or moved it for safekeeping. It is inconceivable to think this a possibility. The Romans would have absolutely no motive for taking the body and if the Jewish leaders had the body why did they not produce it later? In Acts 4, the Jewish authorities were angered and did everything they could to prevent the spread of Christianity. Why would the disciples deceive their own people into believing in a false Messiah when they knew that this deception would mean the deaths of hundreds of their believing friends? More so, if opponents of Christianity (both Jewish and Roman) really knew where the body was, they could have simply presented the body and exposed the Christians to be frauds and ended the faith that caused them so much trouble and anger. Throughout the preaching of the Apostles, the authorities never attempted to refute the Resurrection by producing a body. This theory has little merit.

There has also been the theory that the guards of the tomb fell asleep and the disciples stole the body. This explanation remains an impossibility for several reasons. First, it seems physically impossible for the disciples to sneak past the soldiers and then move a two-ton stone up an incline in absolute silence. Certainly the guards would have heard something. Second, the tomb was secured with a Roman seal. Anyone who moved the stone would break the seal, an offense punishable by death. The depression and cowardice of the disciples makes it difficult to believe that they would suddenly become so brave as to face a detachment of soldiers, steal the body, and then lie about the Resurrection when they would ultimately face a life of suffering and death for their contrived message. Again, myths don't make martyrs. Surely in the face of persecution and martyrdom someone would have cracked. Thirdly, Roman guards were not likely to fall asleep with such an important duty. There were penalties for doing so. The disciples would have needed to overpower them. This is a very unlikely scenario. Finally, in the Gospel of John (a historically reliable document) the grave clothes were found lying there as well as the burial cloth that had been around Jesus' head. The cloth was folded up by itself separate from the linen (20:6-7). There was not enough time for the disciples to sneak past the guards, roll away the stone, unwrap the body, rewrap it in their wrappings, and fold the head piece neatly next to the linen. In a robbery, the men would have flung the garments down in disorder and fled in fear of detection.

It also bears mentioning that none of these theories, with the exception of the soldiers falling asleep (Matthew 28), ever existed within the first century. Most of these theories are from individuals who are literally over a thousand years removed. One should find it odd that such competing theories took that long to develop. If Jesus' tomb was not known, if it had not been found empty, if someone had the body in their possession, or if a group lied about the whole thing and created a hoax then competing theories would have arisen much sooner than a thousand years! The facts remain: Jesus was crucified, died, buried in the known tomb of Joseph of Arimathea, the tomb was discovered empty on Sunday, the disciples were transformed and began preaching the resurrection in Jerusalem almost immediately, and the Christian church was born.

Conclusion:

The best explanation for the evidence that has been presented is that Jesus rose from the dead. Only the resurrection explains the empty tomb, the resurrection appearances, and the existence of the Christian church. No other competing theory can fully explain ALL the evidence that has been presented in this chapter. Thus, the most reasonable answer to the facts is that the resurrection is a historical event complete with eyewitnesses (both friendly and hostile).

Think About It! Richard Swinburne, Probability Calculus, and the Resurrection

Bayes's Theorem is a tool from probability calculus and it is used for assessing how probable a given hypothesis is based upon given evidence. Economists use Bayes's Theorem when making forecasts about consumer spending. Insurance companies and actuaries use Bayes's Theorem to calculate insurance premiums (i.e. to calculate the probability of a claim given certain facts). Bayes's Theorem is also used in medical research. In his textbook, *Judgment and Decision Making*, J. Frank Yates uses an example of a physician determining the probability that a given patient has cancer based upon preliminary observations and facts (i.e. evidence).[18] Thus, Bayes's Theorem is widely used for establishing the probability of an event.

Richard Swinburne is a mathematician and philosopher, as well as a Fellow of the British Academy. Swinburne also taught philosophy at Oxford University in England from 1985 to 2002. In April of 2002 Mr. Swinburne presented a paper before one hundred philosophers at Yale University where he employed Bayes's Theorem to the resurrection of Jesus. This event was also reported in the Saturday, May 11, 2002 edition of the *New York Times.*

In his book *The Resurrection of God Incarnate* Mr. Swinburne provides an incredibly detailed study into the historical evidence regarding Jesus, his teachings, the empty tomb, the post-resurrection appearances, and the existence of the Church to set the stage for concluding by using such evidence in Bayes's Theorem (as presented in his paper at Yale).[19]

Dr. John Warwick Montgomery summarizes Swinburne's argument: Bayes's Theorem asserts that the probability of a hypothesis *h* (here, the facticity of Jesus' resurrection), given evidence *e*, is the initial or prior probability of *h*, multiplied by the probability of the evidence *e*. Expressed as a formula, $Pr(H/E\&B) = [Pr(H/B) \times Pr(E/H\&B)] / Pr(E/B)$, where H is the hypothesis, B is background knowledge (here, natural theology) and E is the evidence acquired by observation (here, the historical case for Jesus' resurrection). Confirmation of the hypothesis occurs, then, insofar as (1) we would expect E to be present if H is true, give B; (2) we would expect H to be true on background evidence alone; and (3) we would not expect to find E unless H were true.[20]

All of Swinburne's work essentially comes down to the following (and please read his 216 page book if you wish for the details): According to Bayes's Theorem using the known facts of consensus of Jesus life and death, there is a 97% chance Jesus rose from the dead. Think about that. What if I told you that you had a 97% chance of winning the lottery if you bought a ticket – would you feel confident enough to go buy a ticket? If I told you that you had a 97% chance of anything based on existing evidence would you consider that solid enough to make a decision? What if someone completed a PhD program in architectural engineering with a grade of 97% in all their classes – would you feel safe in a building they constructed? What if the doctor told you had a 97% of living another 50 years disease free – would you feel pretty good about that?

The evidence is there. Are you going to deal honestly with it?

God Closes In

The list that follows is made up of genuine historical facts that are accepted by nearly all scholars and theologians, whether liberal, conservative, Christian, skeptic, or atheist. In essence, the following facts are rarely, if ever, challenged by any serious and sincere investigator. This list is an excellent common ground to begin a discussion and most of the points have been addressed in some detail within this handbook. A conversation might begin with "These are the facts that we know for sure regardless of our personal beliefs. So, let's deal with the facts and follow where they lead. Are you willing to be open minded about the facts?"

1. The New Testament is the only religious scripture whose complete textual preservation can be established and validated – it is a testable document.
2. The New Testament has its accuracy confirmed by historical methods, archaeology, literary textual criticism, science, and legal reasoning. In fact, the accuracy of the transmission of the New Testament is well over 99%. It is the most superior book from antiquity and a trustworthy historical document.
3. The Bible is the most translated, purchased, memorized, and persecuted book in the history of the world. It has been translated and studied in over 1,700 languages (far more than any other ancient book). This means the New Testament and its content have had individuals investigating it for some 2,000 years in a majority of known languages.
4. The New Testament has had more influence on the world

than any other document; it has molded much of Western civilization. "The Gospels are the very building blocks of our civilization. Without them Giotto would not have painted his frescoes in the Arena Chapel at Padua; Dante would not have written his *Divine Comedy*; Mozart would not have composed his *Requiem*; and Wren would not have built St. Paul's Cathedral. The story and message of these four books – along with the Judaic tradition of the Old Testament – pervade not only the moral convictions of the West, but also our systems of social organization, nomenclature, architecture, literature and education, as well as our rituals of birth, marriage, and death which shape our lives." [1]

5. Jesus existed.
6. Jesus was from Nazareth.
7. Jesus lived a wise and virtuous life.
8. Jesus was a healer and performed unusual feats that his opponents called "sorcery."
9. Jesus died by crucifixion in Palestine under Pontius Pilate during the reign of Tiberius Caesar at Passover time, being accused as the Jewish King.
10. Jesus was buried in a known public tomb of a wealthy person.
11. The tomb was found empty the Sunday after the crucifixion.
12. The disciples of Jesus had real experiences, which they firmly believed were literal post-mortem appearances of the risen and alive Jesus.
13. Jesus' disciples worshiped him as divine.
14. The disciples were radically transformed from frightened skeptics and doubters to bold proclaimers of Jesus' resurrection.
15. The majority of the apostles suffered death because of their firm conviction in Jesus' resurrection. All they had to do to save their lives was to say "Jesus did not rise and he is not God," but they chose death instead. Logic tells us that myths don't make martyrs! Who dies for something they know is a lie?
16. The resurrection was a central teaching of the early church

and Sunday became the primary day of worship because of the belief in the resurrection.

17. James (the skeptical brother of Jesus) converted and became a leader in the early church after the empty tomb discovery.

18. Saul of Tarsus (St. Paul) was once a persecutor of the Christians, but became a zealous convert.

19. 1 Corinthians 15:3-8 is an early creed of the Christian church dating from 33 – 38 AD and displays the very early church's belief in the death, burial, and bodily resurrection of Jesus. This passage eliminates the notion of the bodily resurrection being a legend or later addition to the Christian belief system.

20. The Church today, some 2,000 years after the time of Jesus' life and death, is still centered on his bodily resurrection.

These twenty facts are NOT points for debate – they are established as genuinely historic and accepted within nearly all New Testament scholarship regardless of personal bias. They are facts. Therefore, one must ask, "What are you going to do with the facts?" If one wishes to have an honest and truthful worldview based on a firm foundation then one's worldview must allow for the above twenty facts. Regardless of personal opinion or belief about the resurrection, the New Testament, or Jesus, one's view of reality must incorporate and be consistent with the facts in order to be considered legitimate and honest. As this handbook has shown, the most reasonable explanation to all the facts is that the New Testament is a historical reliable document and that God raised Jesus from the dead. Quite frankly, there is no other explanation that is more reasonable or probable and that deals with the evidence as logically, honestly, and sincerely. For some 2,000 years people have tried to provide an alternative, but there simply is no way around the evidence: Jesus is who he says he was – the very Son of God reconciling the world to himself through his death and bodily resurrection.

C.S. Lewis once described himself as the most reluctant convert in all of England. Lewis did not necessarily want to become a Christian, but as he described it "God closed in on me." It is certainly true that neither this book nor the twenty facts stated above can cause one's heart and soul to believe, but it should at the very least challenge the mind and force one to stop sitting on the fence. Consider the words of Lewis just before his conversion:

> Early in 1926 the hardest boiled of all the atheists I ever knew sat in my room on the other side of the fire and remarked that the evidence for the historicity of the Gospels was really surprisingly good. "Rum thing," he went on... "It almost looks as if it had really happened once." To understand the shattering impact of it, you would need to know the man (who has certainly never since shown any interest in Christianity). If he, the cynic of cynics, the toughest of the toughs, were not – as I would still have put it – "safe," where could I turn? Was there no escape.
>
> ...God closed in on me...I became aware that I was holding something at bay, or shutting something out. Or, if you like, that I was wearing some stiff clothing, like corsets, or even a suit of armor, as if I were a lobster.[2]

Lewis basically had no where else to turn for God had closed in on him. All reason and evidence pointed to Jesus Christ and nowhere else. Whether he liked it or not Christianity was true.

In a more academic way, the German theologian Horst Georg Pohlmann puts the dilemma of God closing in this way:

> Today there is virtually a consensus...that Jesus came on the scene with an unheard of authority, namely the authority of God, with the claim of the authority to stand in God's place and speak to us and to bring us salvation...With regard to Jesus, there are only two possible modes of behavior: either to believe that in him God encounters us, or to nail him to the cross as a blasphemer. There is no third way.[3]

The facts and evidence are there. *There is no third option*: Jesus is who he said he was, namely God in the flesh reconciling the world to himself or else Jesus was a liar and a lunatic. Which is it? What does the evidence honestly say?

Has God closed in on you?

How Firm a Foundation

A hymn by John Rippon, *A Selection of Hymns,* 1787

How firm a foundation, ye saints of the Lord,
Is laid for your faith in His excellent Word!
What more can He say than to you He hath said,
You, who unto Jesus for refuge have fled?

The soul that on Jesus has leaned for repose,
I will not, I will not desert to its foes;
That soul, though all hell should endeavor to shake,
I'll never, no never, no never forsake.

Endnotes

Introduction

1. Kant, Immanuel. *Critique of Pure Reason.* Translated by
   Norman Kemp Smith. St. Martins Press: New York 1965.
   Preface page xxx.

2. Kierkegaard, Soren. *Concluding Unscientific Postscripts.*
   Translated by David F. Swenson and W. Lowrie. Princeton
   University Press 1941. Page 86.

3. Geisler, N.L. *Baker Encyclopedia of Christian Apologetics.*
   Baker Books: Grand Rapids. Page 141.

4. Muller-Hill, Bruno. "Science, Truth, and Other Values,"
   Quarterly Review of Biology, 68, no. 3, September 1993.
   Pages 399-407.

5. Johnson, Phillip E. *Objections Sustained: Subversive Essays
   on Evolution, Law, and Culture.* Intervarsity Press: Downers
   Grove 1998. Pages 156-160.

6. A brief listing of Crossan's TV appearances include the
   following: *Jesus and Paul* on ABC hosted by Peter Jennings
   April 5, 2004; *The Search for Jesus* on ABC hosted by Peter
   Jennings June 26, 2000. *The Selling of the Passion* on ABC's
   Nightline with Ted Koppel on February 25, 2004; *The Last
   Days of Jesus* on NBC's *Dateline* hosted by Stone Philips on
   February 18, 2004; *From Jesus to Christ* a multi-part PBS

special in April 1998. Magazine references include "Why did Jesus Die" in the April 12, 2004 *Time Magazine;* "In Search of Jesus" in the April 8, 1996 *U.S. News and World Report;* "Jesus Christ, Plain and Simple" in the January 10, 1994 *Time Magazine.*

7. Crossan, John Dominic. *Historical Jesus,* 392-396; idem, *Jesus: A Revolutionary Biography.* Harper: San Francisco 1994. Chapter 6.

8. Crossan, John Dominic. *Historical Jesus,* 415-416; idem, *Who Killed Jesus?* Harper: San Francisco 1995. Pages 181-185.

9. Crossan, John Dominic. *Historical Jesus,* Chapter 15; idem *Who Killed Jesus?* Pages 202-208.

10. Crossan, John Dominic. *Historical Jesus,* xii, 404; idem *Jesus,* 161-163; idem "The Historical Jesus," *Christian Century,* December 18, 1991, 1203.

11. Craig, William Lane and Crossan, John Dominic. *Will the Real Jesus Please Stand Up? A Debate between William Lane Craig and John Dominic Crossan.* Baker Books: Grand Rapids 2000. Page 68.

12. Montgomery, John Warwick. *Evidence for Faith.* Probe Books: Dallas 1991. Page 319.

13. Montgomery, John Warwick. *History and Christianity.* Bethany House: Minneapolis. Page 29.

The New Testament Documents: Transmission

1. Sanders, Chauncey. *An Introduction to Research in English Literary History.* MacMillan: New York 1952. Pages 143ff.

2. Montgomery, John Warwick. *History and Christianity.* Page 26.

3. The information regarding the manuscripts is taken from *The Complete Text of the Earliest New Testament Manuscripts* edited by Philip W. Comfort and David. P. Barrett. Baker Books 1999. And *The Origin of the Bible* edited by Philip W. Comfort. Tyndale Publishers: Wheaton 1992.

4. Thiede, Carsten P. and D'Ancona, Matthew. *Eyewitness to Jesus: Amazing New Manuscript Evidence About the Origin of the Gospels.* Doubleday: New York 1996.

5. Thiede, Carsten P. and D'Ancona, Matthew. *Eyewitness to Jesus: Amazing New Manuscript Evidence About the Origin of the Gospels.* Page 46.

6. Thiede, Carsten P. and D'Ancona, Matthew. *Eyewitness to Jesus: Amazing New Manuscript Evidence About the Origin of the Gospels.* Page 140.

7. The information regarding the texts from antiquity, the number of extant manuscripts, etc. is based upon the information in Hall, F.W. *Companion to Classical Texts,* "Manuscript Authorities for the Text of the Chief Classical Writers." Clarendon Press: Oxford. Pages 199ff.

8. Kenyon, Frederic G. *Handbook to the Textual Criticism of the New Testament.* MacMillan and Company: London 1901. Page 4.

9. Hall, F.W. *Companion to Classical Texts,* "Manuscript Authorities for the Text of the Chief Classical Writers." Clarendon Press: Oxford. Pages 199ff.

10. Peters, F.E. *The Harvest of Hellenism.* Simon and Schuster: New York 1971. Page 50.

11. Geisler, Norman L. *Christian Apologetics.* Prince Press: Grand Rapids 2003. Page 308.

12. McDowell, Josh. *The New Evidence That Demands a Verdict.* Nelson: Nashville 1999. Page 43.

13. Greenlee, Harold J. *Introduction to New Testament Textual Criticism.* Eerdmans: Grand Rapids 1977. Page 54.

14. Geisler, Norman L. *Christian Apologetics.* Page 308.

15. Hoffman, R. Joseph. "The Origins of Christianity: A Guide to Answering Fundalmentalists," *Free Inquiry,* 5, Spring 1985. Page 50.

16. Proctor, William. *The Resurrection Report.* Broadman and Holman Publishers: Nashville 1998. Page 187.

The New Testament Documents: Internal Evidence

1. Montgomery, John Warwick. *History and Christianity.* Page 29. Also, Aristotle. *Art of Poetry* 14b – 1461b.

2. Proctor, William. *The Resurrection Report.* Page 93.

3. Proctor, William. *The Resurrection Report.* Page 94.

The New Testament Documents: External Evidence

1. Syme, Sir Ronald. *Tacitus 2 volumes.* Clarendon Press: Oxford 1958. *Annals 15.44.*

2. Much of the information research on Tacitus was based upon that of Habermas, Gary R. *The Historical Jesus: Ancient Evidence for the Life of Christ.* College Press: Joplin 1996.

3. Suetonius, Gaius. *The Twelve Caesars*. Translated by Robert Graves. Penguin: Baltimore 1957. *Claudius 25*.

4. Suetonius, Gaius. *The Twelve Caesars*. Translated by Robert Graves. Penguin: Baltimore 1957. *Nero 16*.

5. Klausner, J. *Jesus of Nazareth*. Collier-MacMillan: London 1929. Page 34. Also, Barnett, Paul. *Is the New Testament Reliable: A Look at the Historical Evidence*. Intervarsity Press: Downers Grove 1986. Page 26.

6. Barnett, Paul. *Is the New Testament Reliable: A Look at the Historical Evidence*. Page 26.

7. Josephus. Josephus: *The Essential Works*. Translated by Paul L. Maier. Kregel: G rand Rapids 1994. Pages 269-270.

8. Josephus. *Josephus: The Essential Works*. Page 281.

9. Pliny. *Letters*. Translated by William Melmoth, rev. by W.M.L. Hutchinson. Harvard University Press: Cambridge 1935. Volume 2, X:96.

10. Habermas, Gary R. *The Historical Jesus: Ancient Evidence for the Life of Christ*. Pages 197-200.

11. Africanus, Julius. *Extant Writings*. XVIII in *Ante-Nicene Fathers*. Edited by Alexander Roberts and James Donaldson. Eerdmans: Grand Rapids 1973. Volume VI page 130.

12. Habermas, Gary R. *The Historical Jesus: Ancient Evidence for the Life of Christ*. Pages 196-197.

13. *The Babylonian Talmud*. Translated by I. Epstein. Soncino: London 1935. Volume 3 *Sanhedrin* 43a page 281.

14. Habermas, Gary R. *The Historical Jesus: Ancient Evidence*

for the Life of Christ. Pages 202-205.

15. Origen. *Contra Celsum*. Volume XIV in the *Ante-Nicene Fathers*.

16. Glueck, Nelson. *Rivers in the Desert: History of Negev*. Farrar, Straus, and Cadahy: New York 1959. Page 31.

17. Albright, W.F. *The Archaeology of Palestine*. Penguin: Baltimore 1960. Pages 127-128.

18. Geisler, N.L. *Baker Encyclopedia of Christian Apologetics*. Page 48.

19. Geisler, N.L. *Baker Encyclopedia of Christian Apologetics*. Page 48.

20. Montgomery, John Warwick. *Tractatus Logico Theologicus*. VKW: Bonn 2002. Page 90.

21. Geisler, N.L. Baker Encyclopedia of Christian Apologetics. Pages 384-385.

22. Blaiklock, Edward Musgrave. *Layman's Answer: An Examination of the New Theology*. Hodder and Stoughton 1968. Page 36. As quoted by Ramsay's book, *St. Paul the Traveler and Roman Citizen*.

23. Albright, William F. Interview with *Christianity Today*, January 18, 1963.

24. Gottschalk, Louis. *Understanding History: A Primer of Historical Method*. Alfred A. Knopf: New York 1969. Pages 53-54. Also, J.P. Moreland uses this method with commentary in Moreland, J.P. *Scaling the Secular City: A Defense of Christianity*. Baker: Grand Rapids 1987. Pages 136-137.

25. Montgomery, John Warwick. *History and Christianity*. Page 29.

So, the New Testament Documents Are Historical. Are They Trustworthy?

1. Greenleaf, Simon. *The Testimony of the Evangelists: The Gospels Examined by the Rules of Evidence*. Kregel: Grand Rapids 1995.

2. Chandler, Walter M. *The Trial of Jesus from a Lawyer's Standpoint*. Federal Book Company 1925. Page 19.

3. Greenleaf, Simon. *The Testimony of the Evangelists: The Gospels Examined by the Rules of Evidence*. Page 34.

4. Montgomery, John Warwick. *Christians in the Public Square*. Canadian Institute of Law, Theology, and Public Policy: Edmonton 1996. Pages 223-250.

5. McCloskey, Patrick L. and Schoenberg, Richard L. Criminal Law Advocacy. Matthew Bender: New York 1984. Volume 5, paragraph 12.01.

6. McCloskey, Patrick L. and Schoenberg, Richard L. *Criminal Law Advocacy*. Volume 5, paragraph 12.03.

7. Quoted from an article in the *Washington Post* quoting the *Palm Beach Post*, April 10, 1996, page 3A. The speech of Justice Scalia was delivered at an event sponsored by the Christian Legal Society held at Mississippi College School of Law.

8. Givens, Richard A. *Advocacy: The Art of Pleading a Cause*. McGraw Hill: 1976. Pages 86-117.

9. Givens, Richard A. *Advocacy: The Art of Pleading a Cause.* Page 12.

10. Montgomery, John Warwick. *Christians in the Public Square.* Page 235.

11. Montgomery, John Warwick. *Christians in the Public Square.* Pages 234-235.

12. Bruce, F.F. *New Testament Documents: Are They Reliable?* Intervarsity Press: Downers Grove 1960 – reprinted 2001. Pages 45-46.

The Resurrection

1. *Interpretation* 20 January 1966, pages 15-26 "On the Analysis of the Confessional Formula in 1 Corinthians 15:3-5.

2. Habermas, Gary R. *The Historical Jesus: Ancient Evidence for the Life of Christ.* Pages 143-170.

3. Edwards, William D. "On the Physical Death of Jesus Christ." *Journal of the American Medical Association*, 255:11, March 21, 1986, page 1463.

4. Dodd, C.H. T*he Apostolic Preaching and Its Development.* Hodder and Stoughton: London 1967. Page 26.

5. Josephus. *Works of Josephus* 4 volumes. Translated by William Whiston. Baker Books: Grand Rapids 1986.

6. Craig, William Lane and Crossan, John Dominic. *Will the Real Jesus Please Stand Up? A Debate between William Lane Craig and John Dominic Crossan.* Page 27. And Robinson, A.T. *The Human Face of God.* Westminster: Philadelphia 1973. Page 131.

7. Althaus, Paul in Pannenberg, Wolfhart. *Jesus-God and Man.*

Printed in the United States
63650LVS00004B/54

9 781594 676710

Hall: Englewood 1990. Pages 134-136.

19. Swinburne, Richard. *The Resurrection of God Incarnate.* Clarendon: Oxford 2003.

20. Montgomery, John Warwick. *Tractatus Logico Theologicus.* Page 124.

God Closes In

1. Thiede, Carsten P. and D'Ancona, Matthew. *Eyewitness to Jesus: Amazing New Manuscript Evidence About the Origin of the Gospels.* Page 153.

2. Lewis, C.S. *Surprised by Joy.* Barnes and Noble Classic: 1955. Page 214.

3. Pohlmann, Horst Georg. *Abriss der Dogmatik.* Translated by William Lane Craig. Patmos: Dusseldorf 1966. Page 230.

SCM Press 1968. Page 100.

8. Craig, William Lane. "The Historicity of the Empty Tomb of Jesus." *New Testament Studies*, 31, 1985. Pages 39-67.

9. Maier, Paul in an interview with *Christianity Today*. "The Empty Tomb as History." Volume XIX, March 28, 1975, page 5.

10. *Independent Press-Telegram*. Long Beach California, Saturday April 21, 1973. Page A10.

11. Van Daaelen, D.H. *The Real Resurrection*. Collins: London 1972. Page 44.

12. Kremer, Jacob. *Die Osterevangelien – Geschichlen um Geschichte*. Quote translated by William Lane Craig. Katholisches Bibelwerk: Stuttgart 1977. Pages 49-50.

13. Lapide, Pinchas. *The Resurrection of Jesus: A Jewish Perspective*. Wipf and Stock Publishers: Eugene 1982 – reprinted 2002. Page 125.

14. Stott, John R.W. *Basic Christianity*. Eerdmans: Grand Rapids 1969. Pages 57-59.

15. Strobel, Lee. *The Case for Christ*. Zondervan: Grand Rapids 1998. Pages 254-255.

16. As quoted in a sermon preached by James McCullen. Sermon posted at www.preachhim.org.

17. Much of the information regarding competing theories has already been covered very well by Pat Zukeran of Probe Ministries. Here I summarize his work. Zukeran has posted his research at www.probe.org/doc/resurrec.html.

18. Yates, J. Frank. *Judgment and Decision Making*. Prentice